THE FORGIVENESS OF SINS

BEAUCHIEF ABBEY LECTURES 2018

The Forgiveness of Sins

Beauchief Abbey Lectures
2018

J. W. Rogerson

BEAUCHIEF
ABBEY·PRESS

Published by Beauchief Abbey Press, May 2021
www.beauchiefabbeypress.org.uk

© Copyright The Estate of the late J. W. Rogerson, 2021
The author's moral rights have been asserted under the Copyright, Designs and Patents Act 1988 to be identified as the author of this work.

ISBN 978-0-9935499-8-4

Scripture quotations from the Authorized (King James) Version of the Bible. Rights in the Authorized Version in the United Kingdom are vested in the Crown. Reproduced by permission of the Crown's patentee, Cambridge University Press.
Scripture quotations from the Revised Standard Version of the Bible, Copyright © 1946, 1952 and 1971, by the Division of Christian Education of the National Council of the Churches of Christ in the USA, reproduced by permission, all rights reserved.

All rights reserved. No part of this publication may be reproduced, copied, stored in a retrieval system, or transmitted, in any form or by any means, without the prior written consent of the copyright holder, nor be otherwise circulated in any form of binding or cover other than that in which it is published and without a similar condition being imposed on the subsequent purchaser.

A CIP catalogue record for this title is available from the British Library.

Cover design by Michael Lindley, Truth Studio, Studio 15, Sum Studios, 1 Hartley Street, Sheffield S2 3AQ. www.truthstudio.co.uk

Printed by www.lulu.com

Foreword

This book attempts to describe God in an old way. It doesn't rely on theories, or suggest that you might think about God in a new way, or become involved in a particular style of religious culture or practice.

The following pages introduce you to how human understanding about God changed 2,000 years ago, and invites you to explore the strange and beautiful dynamic that was created by that change. The subject is the forgiveness of sins. It explores the profound affirmation of forgiveness to people expressed in the teaching, life and death of Jesus and how this brought about an understanding of God that underpins all Christian traditions. The subject of forgiveness brings us into a living, real and important relationship with the living God of the books of the Bible.

The message isn't for religiously minded people, or just for churchgoers. It is for everyone. This is because the issue of forgiveness touches everyone's life. At some point, on a small or very significant issue, we are faced with the question of forgiveness. What is it? How does it relate to me? What does it mean to forgive?

This is the subject of this book.

John Rogerson gave this text as a series of lectures to friends in 2018, and it is the last of his lectures because he died later that year. If this book is your first encounter with John Rogerson, then you can be assured that you are in the company of a very great internationally celebrated scholar, who spent his life studying the biblical traditions of scholarship and the history and interpretation of the Bible. John was also an Anglican priest. During his long career he showed how the Bible, carefully handled, has something profound to say to our lives today, drawing on biblical scholarship, theology, philosophy, sociology, politics, ethics and literature.

He continued this work in retirement and served and taught the small community at Beauchief Abbey, where he brought his gifts and knowledge into service for this little local Anglican church in Sheffield. His friendship was something that many people found transformative, and this friendship, grounded in John's experience and reflection on the Christian offer, is something that continues to resonate very deeply with his friends and readers following his death. We created the Beauchief Abbey Press to allow others to share the remarkable conversations and invitations that came through working with and alongside John. If you enjoy this book you will find others by John, such as *The Kingdom of Heaven, Perspectives on the Passion*, and *The Poet-Prophets of the Old Testament*, that may interest you further, as well as several collections of his remarkable sermons.

The first chapter explores the idea of forgiveness, and notes that forgiveness is not simply a religious idea but a human predicament. Every life faces the problem of forgiveness, because our lives and our relationships are prone to encounters with problems and failure. Also addressed is the question commonly asked of faith traditions, namely, that if a person is honest, sincere and seeks to live a good life, what exactly is the purpose of adding on Christian belief? John explores this question in relation to the context of forgiveness.

The second chapter is about forgiveness in the Old Testament, and John's insights come from a lifetime of study of the Old Testament. We discover that sacrifice in the religion of Ancient Israel was something undertaken in rituals of purification during religious ceremony, and that many writers of the Old Testament literature directly experienced the forgiveness of God in their lives and communities. Forgiveness is not dependent on sacrifice. An understanding of philosophy imbues all of John's writing, and he is careful to emphasise again and again in his work that God is found in relationship, and is not an object. At the end of this chapter we encounter the keen, ancient insight that the human experience of discovering divine relationship is a creative medium,

> 'the love of God does not find its object, but rather creates it'

and it is this creative medium that is expressed in the teaching, life and death of Jesus. Those who personally encountered Jesus found it possible to believe in and be grasped by a relational invitation from God, and the story of this intimacy and confidence continuing after the death of Jesus is the Christian story. The central theme of Jesus and forgiveness forms the third chapter.

A person who experienced this forgiveness and intimacy after the death of Jesus is the remarkable man Paul, and the fourth chapter follows the insights of Paul's sharing of his discovery. Paul understands very deeply that the topic of forgiveness turns the world upside down. The question and practice of forgiveness changes many of the rules, laws, codes and principles by which we ordinarily live, and invites new ways of thinking about our relationships to each other and the world.

The final chapter is a call for excitement in our lives today when we discover how forgiveness shows us what it means to be human. Forgiveness is at the heart of our individual and common life. This book, although written by a great scholar, is not a theory – it is an invitation to you to consider your relationship to the great subject of forgiveness.

This volume is published to coincide with the opening of the Library at Llantwit, a new project in South Wales. A major European centre of learning grew up in Llantwit Major from the sixth century, and there are still great ancient Celtic carved stones to be visited and admired today. Llantwit is a good place to re-discover some of the great intellectual and cultural treasure of the relational Christian traditions. Christian culture flourished and spread 1,500 years ago with a great teacher called Illtud, and we want to help that same tradition today by establishing a new library and cultural centre at Llantwit. One of the central collections in the library, much needed in Britain today, is a collection of books by John Rogerson on the theme of the Kingdom of Heaven.

R. M. Parry
Llantwit Major, 2021

With grateful thanks

Professor John Rogerson's short illness and sudden death in 2018 was a keen loss felt by his family, friends and colleagues. John was working on preparing this text for publication when he died and much gratitude is expressed to his collaborator and friend Fr. Geoffrey Bottoms who has continued with the work, enabling this text to be presented in this edition.

Miss Mary Hodge, another friend of John Rogerson, has set the text and provided excellent administrative support for the Beauchief Abbey Press during its development and growth.

Michael Lindley of Truth Studio in Sheffield has again contributed an exceptional cover design for the volume, and his work continues to make all Beauchief Abbey Press books attractive on the shelf.

Lastly, but by no means least, we thank Mrs Rosalind Rogerson, whose generosity means that copies of this book will be made available as a gift to residents and congregations in Llantwit Major to celebrate the opening of the Library at Llantwit.

Introduction

The suggestion that the subject of the Beauchief Abbey Lent Lectures for 2018 should be *The Forgiveness of Sins* came from several members of the congregation. The suggestion was intended to save me from having to do too much extra work, because some years ago I gave some lectures on the subject of *Perspectives on the Passion*, and these were published by Beauchief Abbey Press.[1] The intention was that speaking about the forgiveness of sins would not involve too much extra work for me. In the event, the preparation of these lectures proved to be time-consuming and absorbing, and I am most grateful for that. There was, however, one difference between this year's lectures and those delivered in previous years. Previously, I wrote formal lectures and read them on the occasions of their delivery, and it was these formal scripts that were later published. This year, I simply provided handouts to which I spoke without a script, intending to record the lectures so that my friend Mary Hodge could transcribe them, and then publish them. However, it became apparent, especially after the lecture on the Old Testament, that much more needed to be said than could be contained in

---

[1] J.W. Rogerson, *Perspectives on the Passion*, Sheffield: Beauchief Abbey Press, 2014.

one brief lecture lasting 40 minutes, and so I decided to give all the lectures orally without recording them, and to write them up extensively during the summer of 2018. The text as it now appears in this book is the result of that extensive writing-up of the lectures. The only exception is with regard to the first lecture, which I did record and which Mary transcribed. It appears as the first chapter in an edited version of the oral form in which it was given.

When I came to deliver the fifth and final lecture, I began by saying that it had occurred to me that I had been lecturing on the wrong subject! I should have been lecturing not on the forgiveness of sins, but on the forgiveness of sinners. This matter will be addressed in the fifth lecture, but it was also a factor that was beginning to shape what was said in some of the earlier lectures, and this should be borne in mind as readers proceed through to the final chapter.

I am grateful, as ever, to the congregation of Beauchief Abbey for inviting me to give the lectures, and also for providing the funding for them to be videoed and available for listening and viewing. As ever, Kieran Collins has done a splendid job in recording and editing the videos.

The forgiveness of sins is a large and crucial subject, and it seems to me strange that it has taken me so long in my life to get around to doing extensive reading and writing on the subject. I hope that readers will find what has been produced helpful and worthwhile.

J. W. Rogerson
Sheffield, 2018

Contents

Foreword	v
With grateful thanks	ix
Introduction	xi
LECTURE 1 What it's all about ...	15
LECTURE 2 Sin and Forgiveness in the Old Testament	29
LECTURE 3 Sin and Forgiveness in the Teaching of Jesus	40
LECTURE 4 Sin and Forgiveness in the Teaching of Paul	55
LECTURE 5 The Forgiveness of Sinners in Today's World	69
APPENDIX 1 Living in the Wilderness: Sermon for Ash Wednesday, 2018	82
APPENDIX 2 A Different Perspective: Sermon for Lent I, 2018	88
Bibliography	94
Biblical References	96
General Index	97
Also by J.W. Rogerson	99

LECTURE 1

What it's all about ...

> I believe in the Holy Ghost; The holy Catholick Church; The Communion of Saints; The Forgiveness of sins; The Resurrection of the body; And the Life everlasting.

The words, 'the forgiveness of sins', occur in the last Article of the Apostles' Creed, and to that extent are as distinctively Christian as the other items in that Creed: the Holy Ghost, the Holy Catholick Church, the Communion of Saints, and so on. But they are different from those words in this respect, that whereas people do not normally talk about the Holy Ghost or the Communion of Saints in secular contexts, people do talk about sins and forgiveness in secular contexts. Perhaps they do not always use those exact words, but the ideas are certainly there, and that creates some interesting problems.

It is not surprising that people should talk about sins and forgiveness in secular contexts. Ever since human society began, when people became self-conscious and lived together in community, there were breaches of certain types of order: damage to a person's property, wars, infringements of taboos, and so on. And, with these breaches of order, there came means, attempted means, of healing the breaches and making people responsible for what they had done. It is a very deep-seated notion that those responsible for offences and breaches of order should in some way be made accountable. In some religious systems, for example in Ancient Egypt, you get a definite reckoning-up of good points and bad points. This was of course for the aristocracy and people who could afford it (in the Book of the Dead, for example), and there is the thought and the hope that as the soul approaches the god in charge of the after-world that good deeds will outweigh the bad deeds.

In our modern society, particularly very recently, there has been a great concern for responsibility; and I am rather glad that we are no longer willing to put up with people running companies who starve the pension funds of the employees, make sure their own pension funds are well topped up, and draw large salaries. It is all to the good, I think, that we are now concerned that people who try to cover up things, whether in the Police or the Health Service, or the churches, or in charities, should be held responsible for these things. But then the question arises, 'How do you compensate for these things? What sort of penalties, what sort of accounting, is appropriate for these things?' One writer, an older theologian whose work I greatly admire, Oliver Quick, almost made the point that, in such circumstances, the word 'forgiveness' is inappropriate if people have actually been in some way punished or paid the cost for their wrongdoings.[2] So, where does forgiveness come in, even though the idea is floating around? It sometimes happens that people are shocked when someone who has lost a relative or friend in some violent incident says that he has forgiven those responsible. An example comes from the Troubles in Northern Ireland, where

---

[2] O. C. Quick, *Doctrines of the Creed. Their Basis in Scripture and Their Meaning Today*, London: Nisbet & Co., 1938, p. 210, 'Forgiveness, strictly speaking, is not a moral conception at all. If an offence be not fully purged, morality requires further penalty; if an offence be fully purged, there is nothing left to be forgiven'.

a man whose son had been murdered, shocked everybody by saying that he had forgiven those who had done it. People did not know what to make of this, or how to understand it. When we accept that people should be held accountable, we are in the realm of the ideas of sin and forgiveness, and yet we are only rather vaguely there, and there is much that is not clear or understood.

What I am going to try to do in these lectures is to ask, 'What does a Christian view of sin and forgiveness amount to in the world in which we live?' The aim is not so that we can then retreat into some sort of pietistic ghetto and let the world get on with itself outside, but so that we can engage constructively from a Christian point of view with some of the sort of things I have been talking about and the concerns that we have. In the first lecture I am only going to be able to introduce the subject and some of the problems, and the subsequent chapters will deal with the Old Testament; the teaching of Jesus; the teaching of Paul; and lastly there will be an attempt to pull it all together and to see where we have got.

As I was wondering where to begin this chapter and how to structure it, it occurred to me that one of the most interesting definitions (if that is the right word) of the word 'sin' comes in a familiar place: the Confession in the Book of Common Prayer, before Morning and Evening Prayer. It is a form of words that goes back to the Prayer Book of 1552, and something which I think has not been matched in any Anglican revision of services since, which seem to take it for granted that everyone knows what 'sin' is, or means. The General Confession goes most of the way without actually ever mentioning the word 'sin', although the word 'sinners' comes towards the end. I shall work through some of the things it says, in order to point up the problems that we will be concerned with.

> Almighty and most merciful Father, We have erred, and strayed from thy ways like lost sheep, We have followed too much the devices and desires of our own hearts, We have offended against thy holy laws, We have left undone those things which we ought to have done, And we have done those things which we ought not to have done, And there is no health in us [which means there is no 'means of salvation'[3]]: But thou, O Lord, have mercy upon us, miserable offenders [and again this does not mean 'depressed' or 'desperate'; it means 'sinners to be pitied'[4]]; Spare thou them, O God, which confess their faults, Restore thou them that are penitent, According to thy promises declared unto mankind in Christ Jesu our Lord: And grant, O most merciful Father, for his sake, That we may hereafter live a godly, righteous, and sober life, To the glory of thy holy name. Amen.

As an Old Testament specialist, I am very interested in the reference to the sheep, 'We have erred and strayed from thy ways like lost sheep', because it resonates with a very deep strain in the Old Testament. We think immediately of Isaiah 53.6, which is also a splendid and well-known chorus in Part 2 of Handel's *Messiah*:

> All we like sheep have gone astray; we have turned every one to his own way; and the LORD hath laid on him the iniquity of us all.

But actually there is a lot more to be said about sheep and shepherds than that. In the Ancient World, the idea of the ruler was very much cast in terms of the shepherd. The Pharaohs of Egypt had on their insignia the shepherd's crook, and the prophets have some fairly harsh things to say about

---

[3] See Stella Brook, *The Language of the Book of Common Prayer*, London: André Deutsch, 1965, p. 47.
[4] Brook, *Language*, pp. 43-44.

shepherds and sheep in the sense of misrule – for example, in Jeremiah 23.1-4:

> Woe to the shepherds who destroy and scatter the sheep of my pasture! says the LORD. Therefore thus says the LORD, the God of Israel, concerning the shepherds who care for my sheep; You have scattered my flock, and have driven them away, and you have not attended to them: Behold, I will attend to you for your evil doings, says the LORD. Then I will gather the remnant of my flock out of all the countries where I have driven them, and I will bring them back to their folds; and they shall be fruitful and multiply. And I will set shepherds over them who will care for them: and they shall fear no more, nor be dismayed, neither shall any be missing, says the LORD.

There are similar sentiments in Ezekiel 34, taken up in the great discourse in John 10, where Jesus says that he is the *Good Shepherd*.

What interests me about the language of sheep and shepherds is this: many worshippers think that wrongdoing is an individual thing – and it is certainly that. Perhaps this is what the writer of the General Confession meant with the words, 'We have erred and strayed like lost sheep', that this is a particularly *individual* thing. But the Old Testament puts these words into a much larger context: that people need to be cared for; and that if they go astray and if they are scattered, it may be their fault, but there may be other things at issue as well. We are reminded that sin is not necessarily just an individual aspect of responsibility; it has a corporate dimension too. It is the fact that, whether we like it or not, we are embedded in a world where there is a corporate wrongness, and it is not the case that we go through life in a neutral world, faced by choices of right and wrong, where there are no other considerations, and that we are wholly responsible for the choices that we make. We *are* responsible for the choices that we make, but we make those choices in the context of a world that is morally ambiguous. So I like the idea of erring and straying like sheep, because it introduces a corporate dimension which is an essential part of any proper *Christian* thinking about what sin means.

We then come on to the next part: 'We have followed too much [notice the words 'too much'] the devices and desires of our own hearts.' Now, there is nothing wrong with devices and desires; there is nothing wrong with human ambition; there is nothing wrong with human achievement; there is nothing wrong with pride in human achievement, depending upon the context in which all this is set. A life lived creatively, imaginatively, in the service of God is one thing; a life lived imaginatively and creatively in the context of values that are narrowly focused on self-interest and disregard for other people – that is quite another matter. And so I take this phrase, 'We have followed too much the devices and desires of our own hearts', to be not a statement against human creativity, imagination and similar things, but language about the context in which they are done.

In my sermon for Ash Wednesday (see pp. 82-7), I was talking about sin as a negative and malevolent power, which we are too weak to resist, partly because of our ignorance, partly because of our weakness, but also because evil is something with which we are allied. I was referring to the remarkable passage in Genesis 4, the story of Cain and Abel and the words spoken by God to Cain when he is minded to kill his brother out of jealousy. 'Sin is crouching at the door; its desire is for you'; and sin is pictured as a kind of animal, crouching to pounce. Sin and wickedness draw their strength from us. They have no strength of their own. You only have to see this when we are tempted to go to war for all kinds of good and proper reasons in defence of the oppressed. As soon as war begins, it opens a window which allows evil to come in and take control and spin events well beyond what we can control. One has only to think of recent events in the Middle East to see the truth of that. There is a dimension of sin and wickedness that any Christian view has to take account of: sin as a mysterious, malevolent negativity, something which surrounds us and sometimes overpowers us, and sometimes with which we find ourselves allied.

Now, as we switch to the next part, 'God's holy laws', we come to something quite different, and something that I find very worrying. We say, Yes, we have offended against thy holy laws. But what are God's holy laws? Where are we going to find them? Well, we could say, perhaps some of them could be found in the Ten Commandments – and, in fact, there are some extremely fine commandments in the Old Testament. Alas! the Church does not really know the Old Testament, and does not take much notice of it. There are some very good Commandments in the Old Testament that have been quietly forgotten, and this points up a problem that I shall expand. Think of the Sabbath. Now, the Sabbath is Friday night to Saturday night; the Sabbath is not Sunday. But the Sabbath is instituted, among other things in the Old Testament, for the protection of the environment and for the protection of animals that might otherwise be exploited. My favourite passage illustrating this, including the Sabbath, comes in Exodus 23.10-12:

> For six years you shall sow your land, and gather in its yield: But the seventh year you shall let it rest and lie fallow; that the poor of your people may eat: and what they leave the wild beasts may eat. You shall do likewise with your vineyard, and with your olive orchard. Six days you shall do your work, but on the seventh day you shall rest: that your ox and your ass may have rest, and the son

of your bondmaid, and the alien [that is, the refugee living with you] may be refreshed.

These things have been conveniently forgotten, I fear, and we only have to look at the recent history of Sunday to see that. I appreciate that Christians in this country are a small minority and there is no reason why their practices on Sundays should be legislated for everybody else. But, fifty years ago, I knew someone, a prominent member of the Church Assembly of the Church of England, a lay reader, who was a member of Surrey County Cricket Club; and when it happened that Surrey County Cricket Club began to play cricket on a Sunday, he felt moved, as a Christian, to write and resign his membership of the club, because it was playing sport on a Sunday. Now, I am not against sport on a Sunday; but there has been an enormous change in recent years in this country, as we go into the seven-day, twenty-four hour week. Sunday is not *quite* like other days yet, though it will be getting there soon. But we have certainly moved away from what might seem a rather outdated, benign idea of time divided up into periods of seven days, so that some people, and animals, will not be exploited by a constant workload; together with the idea that the land may need to rest as well, and that it is *not* the task of humankind to exploit the land all the time. These things have been conveniently forgotten.

Are these God's holy laws? Should we take any notice of them? and what about other things that we find in the Old Testament, such as that we should not charge interest?[5] Think what a big difference that would make! Of course, not much interest is being charged at the moment, but that is not because anyone has made a moral decision about it; it is simply economic necessity that has brought that about. And

---

[5] Exodus 22.25: 'If thou lend money to any of my people that is poor by thee, thou shalt not be to him as an usurer, neither shalt thou lay upon him usury.'

what about the cancelling of debts every seventh year, which comes in Deuteronomy 15. As the year 2000 approached, the so-called 'Jubilee Campaign' – wrongly interpreting Leviticus 25, which doesn't talk about cancelling debt – campaigned that Third World debt should be cancelled. What a different world it would be if we had a different view of debt and indebtedness, and the whole matter of interest was subjected to critical scrutiny, along with the economic system that we have allowed to develop.

The thing that worries me, therefore, about confessing that we have broken God's holy laws is this: What are these laws? Where do they come from? And do we actually rather conveniently forget them if they sound too demanding and too out of line with the world in which we live? Of course, it gets even more difficult when we say, 'We have left undone those things which we ought to have done'. What things ought I to have done? Who is going to tell me what I ought to do, as a Christian? Is my church going to tell me? It raises the whole question of whether there can be, or should be, such a thing as a *Christian* lifestyle and a *Christian* society?

This was an issue that the Broad Church leaders, whom we take very seriously here in the Abbey, F.D. Maurice and Charles Kingsley, certainly addressed. Their nineteenth century was an industrialising nineteenth century, a century that, in movements such as Chartism, was feeling its way towards some kind of representative democracy that hasn't yet been fully realised in this country. They had a vision of a Church and of a society trying to model the values of Christ and his Kingdom. One of the passages from Maurice's sermons that I love is one in which he says that it is one of the jobs of the clergy to tell people that every calling that they exercise, in industry, commerce, or whatever else, is something that is consecrated to God; and that there are not just some offices, such as that of the clergy, which are consecrated, but all callings are consecrated to God, with implications for those offices.[6] That is a very noble vision, described in Maurice's great book, *The Kingdom of Christ*.[7] More recently, that vision was articulated by William Temple in his book, *Christianity and Social Order*,[8] published in 1942; and it is interesting that Temple was very strong on restricting the use of interest. He argued that, from a Christian point of view, the only credible interest that could or should be charged was the cost of administration, plus a very small percentage, but certainly not so that money could be made by lenders. I hate it when I hear financial advisers talking about 'getting your money to work for you', because that is the one thing it doesn't do! I rather like the distinction made by a politician a long time ago between those who make money and those who earn money.[9]

Now, what do we do here? If I am a Christian, what does that mean for the way I live my life? If I am a Christian, does that mean I should send my children to state schools, and not to private schools? If I am a Christian, does that mean I should use the NHS and not private health? If I am a Christian, does that mean I should read *Private Eye* and *The Guardian*, and not *The Spectator* and *The Daily Telegraph*? Am I simply foisting here my own sort of middle class academic prejudices? Should I shop at the Co-op, rather than Tesco? (Actually, I do shop at

---

[6] F. D. Maurice, *The Patriarchs and Lawgivers of the Old Testament*, London: Macmillan, 1892, p. 216.
[7] F. D. Maurice, *The Kingdom of Christ*, 2 vols, London: James Clarke (reprint), 1959.
[8] William Temple, *Christianity and Social Order*, Harmondsworth: Penguin, 1942.
[9] See Temple, *Christianity*, p. 116. A massive history of money, including the history of interest, is provided in K.-H. Brodbeck, *Die Herrschaft des Geldes. Geschichte und Systematik*, Darmstadt: Wissenschaftliche Buchgesellschaft, 2009. Temple gives a very brief overvue in *Christianity*, pp. 45-49.

the Co-op!) But I don't get the impression from the churches that anybody is helping me, or anybody else, to see what a Christian lifestyle would be like, if there is such a thing. And if there isn't a Christian lifestyle, that has some serious implications that I shall come to in a minute. But I want to say this: that we should perhaps engage more responsibly with the Christian tradition on this matter. Calvin is not one of my favourite theologians; but his exposition of the Ten Commandments raises serious questions about how Christians should conduct themselves. This is what he has to say in his *Institutes* about the Eighth Commandment, 'Thou shalt not steal':

> [God] sees the long train of deception by which the man of craft begins to lay nets for his more simple neighbour, until he entangles him in its meshes – sees the harsh and cruel laws by which the more powerful oppress and crush the feeble – sees the enticements by which the more wily baits the hook for the less wary, though all these escape the judgment of man, and no cognisance is taken of them. Nor is the violation of this commandment confined to money, or merchandise, or lands, but extends to every kind of right; for we defraud our neighbours to their hurt if we decline any of the duties which we are bound to perform towards them. If an agent or indolent steward wastes the substance of his employer, or does not give due heed to the management of his property; if he unjustly squanders or luxuriously wastes the means entrusted to him; if a servant holds his master in derision, divulges his secrets, or in any way is treacherous to his life or his goods; if, on the other hand, a master cruelly torments his household, he is guilty of theft before God; since everyone who, in the exercise of his calling, performs not what he owes to others, keeps back, or makes away with what does not belong to him.[10]

---

[10] John Calvin, *Institutes of the Christian Religion*, Book Two, Chapter VIII, Florida: Macdonald (no date), p. 208.

In other words, there are many ways of transgressing this commandment that have implications for Christian living, and obeying 'God's holy laws'; and there is a lot more of the same vein in Calvin's exposition of the Ten Commandments which would repay careful study.

If we say that we do not know whether there is, or whether there can be, such a thing as a *Christian* lifestyle, lived in the context and awareness of sin and forgiveness, there is the danger that the idea of forgiveness of sins will be trivialised and privatised to the point of meaninglessness. In other words, we shall be left with a view of sin that reduces our sin simply to losing our temper, being bad-natured, doing petty things; and we mustn't forget the stress that is laid upon the sexual side of things. People in the outside world might think that the only sins that Christians are concerned about are sexual transgressions. We privatise our behaviour, and we let the world go on outside, and we think that the Church is there simply to be an ecclesiastical laundry in which we can launder the stained linen of our individual transgressions. And all this is to make a mockery of the fact that the words 'the forgiveness of sins' are embedded in a Creed which is about God and what he has done in Jesus Christ.

Years ago, a Methodist minister called David Head wrote a rather amusing little book, entitled, *He sent Leanness*, and it contains some extremely hard-hitting prayers. How about this version of the General Confession?

> Benevolent and easy-going Father; we have occasionally been guilty of errors of judgement. We have lived under the deprivations of heredity and the disadvantages of environment. We have sometimes failed to act in accordance with common sense. We have done the best we could in the circumstances; And have been careful not to ignore the common standards of decency; And we are

glad to think we are fairly normal. Do thou, O Lord, deal lightly with our infrequent lapses. Be thine own sweet Self with those who admit that they are not perfect; According to the unlimited tolerance which we have a right to expect from thee. And grant as an indulgent Parent that we may rather continue to live a harmless and happy life and keep `our self-respect.[11]

This is cynical and hard-hitting, but it strongly expresses the point that is bothering me here. There are people I call 'citizens with active social consciences' and I am grateful that there are such people. Let there be as many as possible! But what do we say to such people with active social consciences when they ask us, 'What difference does being a Christian make?'

The phrase, 'the forgiveness of sins', comes towards the end of the Apostles' Creed, and that creed is about Jesus Christ as the One who reveals God in his birth, ministry, death, and resurrection; and what we have to ask ourselves is, 'What is all this about?' The answer is that it is about God's costly involvement in the world to the extent of a Cross; and as we approach Holy Week, Good Friday and Easter, we think again about that costly involvement. Has that costly involvement happened simply so that our private misdemeanours can somehow be expunged and our conscience salved in the sight of God? Or is there something much more fundamental? In fact, to trivialise sin is to trivialise salvation; to realise the cost of salvation is to take seriously why it was and is needed. Salvation is about God coming into the world to re-create it, to re-create those who inhabit it and who in so many ways mar and destroy it. It is a mighty work of re-creation, of redemption, of renewal, of opening up the future, not only here but beyond this world. It is a mighty work. And only by

---

[11] David Head, *He sent Leanness: A Book of Prayers for the Natural Man*, London: Epworth Press, 1959, p. 19.

realising the cost of salvation and by taking it seriously can we begin to understand what Christians should mean by forgiveness and sin. This is nothing less than an exercise in rediscovering the Gospel, in speaking to our world not in some narrow or simplistic way, but stating it as something that carries intellectual, spiritual, and aesthetic conviction. These lectures will to try to explore the meaning of sin and forgiveness in a way that hopefully will make sense of why the words, 'the forgiveness of sins', occur in a creed, a creed about Jesus Christ, Jesus Christ who reveals God, Jesus Christ who reveals a God involved in his world and concerned with it, concerned with its wickedness, concerned to overcome and transform it through forgiveness.

My final word is this. What would I say to one of those people I describe as 'a citizen with an active social conscience' if I were asked, 'What difference does it make to be a Christian?'? I would reply 'I believe in the forgiveness of sins'.

CHAPTER 2

Sin and Forgiveness in the Old Testament

The study of sin and forgiveness in the Old Testament is complicated by two widely-held and completely false ideas. The first is the idea that the forgiveness of sins in the Old Testament is entirely connected with sacrifices, sacrifices which were anticipatory or illustrative of the sacrifice of Christ on the Cross. The second mistaken idea is that God was unable to forgive sins until Jesus had died on the Cross in order to pay the penalty for human sins. I remember, even before I was a student, having an argument with an evangelical clergyman, who insisted that no-one could be forgiven before Christ died. I quoted to him the words from Psalm 103.12: 'As far as the east is from the west, so far hath he set our transgressions from us'. The clergyman insisted that these words were not from the Psalms but from Isaiah (unfortunately, I didn't have a Bible to hand to show him the passage), that they were therefore a prophecy of the death of Christ, and that they in no way invalidated the point on which he was insisting.

I said above that the first mistaken idea was the idea that the forgiveness of sins in the Old Testament was *entirely* connected with sacrifices. Obviously, there is a good deal of material in the Old Testament about sacrifices as such. This material is important, and I shall say something about it. But it must be noted at the outset, that the sacrificial system of the Old Testament did not deal with the moral offences of individual Israelites. Some sacrifices had to do with what I shall describe shortly as liminal events. There are also two other important types of material in the Old Testament that have to do with forgiveness that must be considered, in addition to the material about sacrifice. These passages are the Psalms and the prophetic books, but also the many narratives of the Old Testament that deal with God's relationship with individuals and with the Israelite people.

It was Bishop Westcott, who, in his commentary on the Greek text of the Letter to the Hebrews, after an exhaustive survey of the sacrifices of the Old Testament, concluded:

> It is necessary to observe that the range of Levitical atonements was very narrow. They were confined to
>
> (a) Bodily impurity,
> (b) Ceremonial offences
> (c) Sins of ignorance
> (d) Certain specified offences: Lev. vi. 1, 7; xix.20.
>
> They did not deal with moral offences as such; they had no relief for 'high-handed sins'. Here the voice of the Psalmist and Prophet met the heart-broken penitent with promises which the Law could not give.[12]

There are, in fact, many sacrifices in the Old Testament that have nothing to do with sin or transgression, such as the daily offerings in the Temple, those made by individuals as thank-offerings, or when vows are made, or by the community

---

[12] B. F. Westcott, *The Epistle to the Hebrews. The Greek Text with Notes and Essays*, London: Macmillan, 1892, pp. 288-289.

before going to war, or sacrifices in connection with such events as the consecration of priests or the rehabilitation of lepers.

Ancient Israel, in common with almost every other society that has been studied by social anthropologists, had a sacrificial system that derived from the liminal situations that confronted individuals and groups.[13] Liminal situations were those on the boundaries between life and death. They embraced birth, illness and death, but also natural disasters, as well as catastrophes arising from war and violence. These situations had in common the fact that they defied explanation or understanding, and could only be coped with by symbolic actions, which usually involved the costly offering of animals, or food and drink, as a 'gift' to whatever unseen agencies were thought to need appeasement. Blood was an important factor in many such offerings, as blood occupied a key position between life and death. It was present in the birth of children and in the menstruation of women, and yet it was associated with death if blood was lost through injury. The Old Testament held that 'the life of the flesh is in the blood' and the strongest penalties were prescribed for anyone who ate or drank blood (Leviticus 17.10-14). An unburied dead body was a liminal object, and contact with it defiled a person such that an elaborate ritual was prescribed in the Old Testament to provide 'medicated water' to enable the defiled person to wash away the defilement (Numbers 19). Of supreme liminal significance was the sacred, the realm of the divine and of the places, objects and appliances that mediated between the

---

[13] See the general account in J. H. M. Beattie, 'On Understanding Sacrifice' in M. F. C. Bourdillon, M. Fortes (eds.), *Sacrifice*, London: Academic Press, 1980, pp. 29-44. See my own essay in the same volume 'Sacrifice in the Old Testament: Problems of Method and Approach', pp. 45-60, reprinted in J. W. Rogerson, *Cultural Landscapes and the Bible. Collected Essays*, Sheffield: Beauchief Abbey Press, 2014, pp. 72-92.

profane and the sacred. The sacred could not be approached without sacrificial offerings, which usually involved the shedding and sprinkling of the blood of sacrificial animals.

These aspects of sacrifice were not unique to Ancient Israel. What was unique was the belief that the sacrificial system had been commanded by God to Moses.[14] This brought the sacrificial system into the narrative of God's dealings with Ancient Israel and his Covenant with them, and it is in this narrative of the Covenant of God's dealings with his people that the essential teaching about sin and forgiveness in the Old Testament is to be found. It explains Westcott's statement that the Levitical ordinances did not deal with moral offences as such. However, the fact that a sacrificial system existed in Ancient Israel and persisted to the destruction of the Second Temple, a system linked to the dangers of approaching the sacred, and the mysterious nature of the liminal, formed a transcendent background to God's personal dealings with his people and individuals within it. These personal dealings will be dealt with at length shortly. First, however, the objection must be considered that there was an Old Testament sacrifice for the forgiving of moral offences, namely the ritual of the Day of Atonement (Leviticus 16).

In fact, the ritual of the Day of Atonement was not a sacrifice. No animal was slaughtered so that its blood could be shed in connection with the remission of sins. It is true that animals were sacrificed in order to allow the High Priest to cross the boundary into the realm of the sacred, so that he could carry out the injunctions of the Day of Atonement. However, the essential part of the ceremony was a transference rite. The sins of the community were confessed over the head of the

---

[14] See the long narrative beginning in Exodus 34 and extending through Leviticus and Numbers.

scapegoat, which was then led into the wilderness and left there. According to one tradition, it was pushed over a precipice to its death;[15] but pushing an animal over a precipice, if this is what happened, is not the same as a ritual in which an animal is slaughtered and its blood is sprinkled on an altar of purification. The Day of Atonement was essentially an act in which sin was symbolically removed from the midst of the congregation.[16] It was not a sacrifice in the strict sense, and in no way proves the view that in the Old Testament, in order for sins to be forgiven, a sacrifice had to be offered.

The foundational narratives of the Old Testament centre on particular persons such as Abraham, Jacob, Moses and David. Although the first three of these characters were certainly historical figures, we know little about where and when they lived; and it is the cultural memory of Ancient Israel that has given them a narrative existence that has drawn upon a wide variety of traditions and experience of encounter with the God of Israel. These have produced narratives that reflect profoundly on the divine initiative and on the complicated responses of people at one and the same time thankful, sympathetic, loyal, rebellious, fearful, ignorant, selfish and fragile. David stands on the threshold of recorded history, but he, too, is the product of cultural memory; of especial importance, as I shall argue, is the belief that he was the author of many of the Psalms.

The narratives about Abraham and Sarah in the Book of Genesis are fine examples of the divine initiative and the uncertain human response. The couple are in their nineties,

---

[15] Mishnah Tractate *Yoma* 6.6, in H. Danby, *The Mishnah*, Oxford: Oxford University Press, 1933, p. 170.
[16] See D. Davies, 'An Interpretation of Sacrifice in Leviticus,' *Zeitschrift für die alttestamentliche Wissenschaft* 89 (1977), pp. 387-399.

childless, and with no hope of descendants. God promises that they will become the parents of a great nation (Genesis 12.1-2). However, Abraham finds it difficult to understand this promise, and he tries various ways to bypass it and gain descendants through his own efforts. One such effort is to have a child, Ishmael, through his wife's servant Hagar (Genesis 16.1-3). Again, on two occasions when Abraham finds himself at the mercy of powerful foreign rulers, and for the sake of his own safety, he denies that Sarah is his wife at all (Genesis 12.9-20; 20.1-18). This is hardly commendable behaviour on the part of someone who has been singled out to become the ancestor of a people through whom God will bring blessing to the nations of the world.

The traditions about Jacob, the father of the sons who later form the twelve tribes of Israel, show him to be a trickster, who tricks his elder brother out of his birthright and his father's blessing, blatantly lying in the process. Again, he hardly seems to be the ideal person to carry further God's promises to a people that will bring blessings to the nations. Paradoxically, it is God's way to use the ungodly to further his purposes. In the story of Jacob, two accounts are pivotal in the narrative. The first is his dream at Bethel while he is on the run from his brother Esau (Genesis 28.10-22). He has a vision of God, and this is the first time that God has seriously entered into his existence in the narrative. God renews his promises to Abraham's descendants through Jacob, although Jacob's response is hardly worthy of the promises. The second encounter with God occurs on the eve of Jacob's reunion with his estranged brother. A mysterious wrestling match takes place at the river Jabbok, in which Jacob wrestles with a man who appears to be not only an angel but in some sense the presence of God himself (Genesis 32.23-32). While this story is mysterious and open to many different interpretations,[17] the most important thing about it is the prayer that Jacob prays before the wrestling match, a prayer which shows how much God's dealings with Jacob have changed him into something more worthy of being God's servant:

> Jacob said, O God of my father Abraham, and God of my father Isaac, the LORD which saidst unto me, Return unto thy country, and to thy kindred, and I will deal well with thee: I am not worthy of the least of all the mercies, and of all the truth, which thou hast shewed unto thy servant; for with my staff I passed over this Jordan; and now I am become two bands. Deliver me, I pray thee, from the hand of my brother, from the hand of Esau: for I fear him, lest he will come and smite me, and the mother with the children. And thou saidst, I will surely do thee good, and make thy seed as the sand of the sea, which cannot be numbered for multitude. (Genesis 32.9-12)

In the narrative about Moses the divine initiative is expressed in the story of his birth (Exodus 2.1-10). The Pharaoh has ordered the killing of all Hebrew baby boys, and the mother of Moses places him in a special ark made to float, and as it floats down the Nile it is seen by Pharaoh's daughter. She rescues the ark and the baby within it, and Moses is able to grow up in the safety of the Egyptian court. In the incident of the burning bush (Exodus 3.1-20), God speaks to Moses, says that he has seen the plight of his people in slavery, and commissions Moses to go to Pharaoh and demand their release. Moses is reluctant to accept his divine mission, rather as Jeremiah is later very reluctant to accept his mission. Indeed, the story of Moses leading his people out of slavery and through the wilderness shows the perils of heeding the call of God to be

---

[17] See my 'Wrestling with the Angel. A Study in Literary Hermeneutics' in A. Loades *et al.* (eds.), *Hermeneutics, the Bible and Literary Criticism*, London: Macmillan, 1992, pp. 131-144. Reprinted in J. W. Rogerson, *Cultural Landscapes and the Bible*, pp. 285-302.

his servant. The people he has led out of slavery continually criticise him and the God who was responsible for their freedom, and Moses is eventually denied entry to the Promised Land because of the waywardness of the people. During the journey through the wilderness, the sacrificial system attributed to him is revealed by God; and as I have said above, the main purpose of this system is to enable society to function harmoniously by the symbolic removal of evil and wickedness from its midst. The sacrifices do not atone for individual acts of wrongdoing. Many such offences are dealt with simply by being subject to the death penalty.

The importance of the Wilderness Wanderings narratives, which begin in the Book of Exodus and continue through Leviticus and Numbers into Deuteronomy, is that they show a God who is very different from the God of Calvinism, as popularly understood: that God is essentially a judge in whose court mankind as a whole stands guilty and only pardonable because Christ has suffered on behalf of sinful humanity and satisfied the divine wrath. The Wilderness Wanderings narratives do not compromise the holiness and transcendence of God, neither do they suggest that evil and wickedness are in any way less serious than they are. What these narratives show is that God is constantly engaging mercifully with his people. He is aware of their frailty and of the dangers that they face. He defends them against their enemies, and feeds them in their hunger. He bears with their constant rejections of him and their constant refusal to be in any way grateful for what he has done for them. It is in the context of narratives such as these that we must understand what the Old Testament is saying about sin and forgiveness. In the Old Testament they occur within the context of a covenant, a relationship which God has specially created and which the stubbornness and ingratitude of the people he has redeemed cannot break or outlast. It is no accident that a psalm such as Psalm 136, which recounts the events of the redemption from slavery and the divine leading to the Promised Land, contains the refrain, 'For his mercy endureth for ever', where the Hebrew word *hesed*, translated as 'mercy', means unfailing and covenant love.

In I Samuel 13.14, David is described as 'the man after God's own heart', and it is David who rescues the people after they have been defeated by the Philistines, who founds Jerusalem, and becomes the type for God's ideal future ruler. However, in the narrative, David, 'the man after God's own heart', is deeply flawed, as is shown by the story of his adultery with Bathsheba, and his attempts to cover up his guilt by arranging for her husband to be killed in battle (II Samuel 11). It is interesting that in the narrative where Nathan the prophet confronts David with his wrongdoing and David confesses his sin, Nathan declares that God has 'put away' his offence (II Samuel 12.13). David is forgiven, and there is no need for any penalty to be paid in order for this to happen, although David has to suffer the disintegration of relationships within his family.

The most remarkable thing about the David tradition is the later belief that he is the author of most or many of the psalms. Some of the titles, even if they belong to a later tradition, link psalms with incidents in the life of David: Psalm 51, the most sublime confession of human frailty and need for forgiveness in the whole Bible, is explicitly linked to David's repentance when Nathan confronted him with his adultery and his attempts to cover it up. The David portrayed in the Psalms is a very human and fragile figure, assailed by doubts and uncertainties, threatened by his enemies within and without, and deeply aware of his need for God's grace and forgiveness.

It is no accident that in Christian worship and private spirituality the Psalms have played a central part in helping congregations and worshippers to express their need for God's grace and forgiveness, and to be assured that their requests have been met.

A word also needs to be said about the many passages in the prophets which speak of God's mercy and forgiveness. Representative are the following words that come at the end of the Book of Micah:

> Who is a God like unto thee, that pardoneth iniquity, and passeth by the transgression of the remnant of his heritage? he retaineth not his anger for ever, because he delighteth in mercy. He will turn again, he will have compassion upon us; he will subdue our iniquities; and thou wilt cast all their sins into the depths of the sea. (Micah 7.18-19)

The proper setting for understanding sin and forgiveness in the Old Testament is not the law court, or even the Temple altar and the bringing of animal sacrifices. The proper context for understanding sin and forgiveness is the family, and many texts in the Old Testament witness to that fact. At the beginning of Isaiah, God complains through the prophet,

> I have nourished and brought up children, and they have rebelled against me. (Isaiah 1.2)

In Psalm 103 come these words:

> Yea, like as a father pitieth his own children: even so is the Lord merciful unto them that fear him. For he knoweth whereof we are made: he remembereth that we are but dust. The days of man are but as grass: for he flourishes as the flower of the field. For as soon as the wind goeth over it, it is gone: and the place thereof shall know it no more.

> But the merciful goodness of the Lord endureth for ever and ever upon them that fear him: and his righteousness upon children's children. (Psalm 103.13-17).

Sins in the Old Testament damage the relationship between God and his people and between God and individuals, but forgiveness is not a matter of meeting judicial requirements, but of restoring the broken relationships, and this is something that God in his mercy is prepared to do. It was he, after all, according to the witness of the Old Testament, who established the covenant relationship in the first place.

In the 28th Thesis of his Heidelberg Disputation, Martin Luther declared that 'the love of God does not find its object, but rather creates it.'[18] This is profoundly true of the story of God choosing the Israelites to be his special people, and is fundamental for understanding what the Old Testament teaches us about sin and forgiveness.

---

[18] See J. Dillenberger, *Martin Luther. Selections from his Writings*, New York: Anchor Books, 1961, p. 503.

CHAPTER 3

Sin and Forgiveness in the Teaching of Jesus

The interpretation of Jesus's teaching on the forgiveness of sins, as presented in the New Testament, is affected by a matter of text and translation. Anglican, Roman Catholic, and Free Church worshippers in England, using the traditional form of the Lord's Prayer, are used to praying the words, 'Forgive us our trespasses'. In Presbyterian churches in Scotland and North America, worshippers pray, 'Forgive us our debts'. The version with 'trespasses' goes back to the First Prayer Book of Edward VI, published in 1549. It depended on Tyndale's translation, 'Forgive us our trespasses'. The traditional form used by Presbyterians is that found in the Authorized Version of the Bible, 'Forgive us our debts'. This translation almost certainly followed that of the Geneva Bible of 1560, 'Forgive us our dettes'. Of the two possibilities, 'forgive us our debts' more accurately renders the Greek of Matthew 6.12 which has the word *opheilamata*.

Exactly why Tyndale used the rendering 'trespasses' is not clear. Luther's translation, which Tyndale valued highly, used the word *Schuld*, which has the double sense of debts and guilt. Tyndale certainly knew that the Greek verbal stem *opheilon* had to do with debts and obligation, as is seen by his translations elsewhere (e.g., Luke 11.4). Tyndale could also have used the word 'sins', as he did in translating *hamartia* in Luke's version of the Lord's Prayer at 11.4. However, Luke had followed this up in the second part of the Fifth Petition of the Lord's Prayer with the words, 'For we also forgive everyone that is *indebted to us*', where indeed the Greek verbal stem is *opheilon*. Perhaps Tyndale meant 'trespasses' to be a compromise between 'debts' and 'sins', although it leaned closer to 'sins' than 'debts'. Lohse is of the opinion that Luke had 'debts' more in mind than 'sins'.[19]

The usual scholarly explanation of why Luke used the word 'sins' is that Jesus taught the prayer in Aramaic, and he used the word *hova* which has the sense of debt and sin. This was interpreted as 'debts' by Matthew's tradition and by 'sins' in Luke's tradition. Even so, as just noticed, Luke's translation continues with the words, 'For we also forgive everyone that is *indebted to us*'. In view of this, it is highly regrettable that modern liturgical versions of the Lord's Prayer read, 'Forgive us our sins, as we forgive those who sin against us'. Biblical scholarship has been ignored in the interests of superficial modernisation.

The difference between 'debts' and 'sins' is profound, a topic explored in great depth in Lohmeyer's book on the Lord's Prayer.[20] In favour of the Greek reading of 'debts' in Matthew is the fact that when Jesus illustrated his teaching on forgiveness, he used parables drawn from the world of

---

[19] Bernhard Lohse, *A Short History of Christian Doctrine from the First Century to the Present*, translated by F. Ernest Stoeffler, Philadelphia: Fortress Press, 1963.

[20] Ernst Lohmeyer, *Das Vater-unser*, Göttingen: Vandenhoeck & Ruprecht, 1947. English version: *The Lord's Prayer*, translated by J. Bowden, London: HarperCollins, 1965.

indebtedness. In answer to Peter's question of how many times he should forgive his brother, Jesus tells the Parable of the Unforgiving Servant, who, having been forgiven debts equivalent to fifteen years' wages for a labourer, refuses to remit a debt equivalent to a hundred days' wages for a fellow servant (Matthew 18.23-35).

Again, on being criticised by a Pharisee for accepting the ministrations of a woman whom Jesus had forgiven and who had a reputation as a 'sinner', Jesus tells the Parable of the Two Debtors (Luke 7.36-50). There are also other parables drawn from the world of money, such as the Talents (Matthew 25.14-30) and the Pounds (Luke 19.12-27), and the Dishonest Steward (Luke 16 1-9). Most important of all is the Parable of the Prodigal Son and the Elder Brother, where the errant son becomes indebted to his father by wasting his share of the inheritance (Luke 15.11-32).

The main difference between a sin and a debt is that a debt is more clearly a default within a relationship. A sin might be understood in the same way, as a violation of a law, the breaking of which dishonoured the lawgiver or the system that maintained it; but this is arguably a more indirect way of being disloyal within a relationship than defaulting on what is owed to a person financially. In the Parable of the Unforgiving Servant, there are direct, personal relationships between the master and his servant, and between the unforgiving servant and his unfortunate victim.

Lohmeyer makes the point that the idea of debt and obligation can be extended to human dependence upon God for life, food and clothing.[21] Obligation has a much wider sense than sin, and the prayer for forgiveness for being disloyal in regard to

---

[21] Lohmeyer, *Das Vater-unser*.

human obligations to God goes to the very heart of the relationships between God and humanity. It also goes to the heart of the Old Testament view of sin and forgiveness.

In the prophetic books, the complaint against the Israelites is not so much that of law-breaking as that of disloyalty within a close relationship:

> I have nourished and brought up children, and they have rebelled against me. The ox knoweth his owner, and the ass his master's crib: but Israel doth not know, my people doth not consider. (Isaiah 1.2-3)

Forgiveness in the Old Testament, as I said in the previous chapter, is not a matter of atoning for offences, but of restoring the relationship between a God who speaks of 'my people' and complains about their disloyalty. Jeremiah sums up the situation vividly:

> For my people have committed two evils; they have forsaken me the fountain of living waters, and hewed them out cisterns, broken cisterns, that can hold no water. (Jeremiah 2.13)

We could well paraphrase the prayer, 'Forgive us our debts', with the words, 'Forgive us for being disloyal'.

To return to the distinction between forgiveness as atonement for an offence, and forgiveness as the cancellation of debts, it will be necessary to examine in detail the implications of the contexts in which the two different approaches function. In the case of forgiveness as atonement, the language and imagery are drawn from the law-court and criminal practice. In the case of forgiveness as cancelling debts, the language and imagery are drawn from a wider background, ranging from private and intimate transactions within the family and friends to the formal world of mortgages and hire purchase.

Only some of the relationships within the remission of debts are suitable for understanding the teaching of Jesus. Mortgages and hire purchase are not suitable.

The striking thing about the law-court setting is that it is necessarily *impersonal*. If the accused person has offended the judge, that judge will not be able to hear the case. The accused person has violated laws, laws designed to protect the person and property of others and to ensure that the course of everyday life functions in an orderly manner. Therefore, the judge acts, not within the context of a relationship, but in order to uphold the justice that that breaking of the code has broken. In a theological context, the accused person, when found guilty of the offence, does not have the wherewithal to meet whatever penalties are imposed, at which point he or she draws upon the 'price of sin', which was paid by Christ on the Cross. The judge releases the guilty person, who remains guilty.

Perhaps I have described this 'penal substitution' view of atonement unfairly and crudely. I would certainly be the first person to acknowledge that it has helped many people into faith. It has helped them to see that forgiveness is a costly business, and that the Loving Father has himself borne this cost through the death of his Son. However, my concern here is to explore the difference between forgiveness as an 'atoning for' and forgiveness as the remission of debt.

Relationships are fundamental to the idea of forgiveness as cancellation or remittance of debts. It is true that in today's world people can owe money to organisations or institutions. This was not the case in the time of Jesus. His parables assume that people are indebted to other people. The cancellation of debts involves one person not insisting on his right to receive repayment of a loan or its equivalent. The cancellation of debts is an act of generosity on the part of the lender and immediately removes the whole matter from the realm of law to that of gracious and kindly dealing, for which and against which there is and can be no law. The default of the borrower mars or damages the relationship within which the loan was made. The act of cancelling debt repairs the relationship.

In the light of this let's look again at the familiar words in the Lord's Prayer which have been translated, 'And forgive us our trespasses, as we forgive them that trespass against us'. It is easier to say what this cannot mean than what it must mean. It cannot mean that we forgive our debtors in the same way that God remits our debts to him. This makes us equal to God and assumes what we cannot know, namely how and why he remits our debts. It cannot mean that God remits our debts because we remit debts owed by others to us. This would make God's remitting dependent upon our remitting: a bizarre inversion of the relationship between the creator and creature! Unfortunately, this conclusion can be drawn by a false logical deduction from the words of Jesus at the end of the Parable of the Unforgiving Servant, 'If you do not forgive those who trespass against you, neither will your Heavenly Father forgive you your trespasses.'

The petition might mean, paraphrasing, 'We pray you to forgive us our trespasses; we also forgive those who trespass against us': but in this case it is hard to see what point is being made, or what this part of the petition adds to the main part, 'Forgive us our trespasses'. If we are to make sense of the words, 'as we forgive them that trespass against us', we must put them in the context of shared conventions that are fundamental to being human: to being 'bound in the bundle of life' (I Samuel 25.29). One such convention is that of loyalty, in the sense of a readiness to keep a promise made, even if something else has come up in the meantime, which we would much rather do than keep the promise.

The German sociologist Niklas Luhmann calls these 'symbolically generalised media of communication'. Fortunately, behind the formidable jargon lie well-known situations of everyday life. I have given the example of being loyal to a promise when we would much rather be doing something else. Luhmann's example is the expectation of truthfulness in the field of academic research, but he extends the example to include mediums of exchange, i.e., money and property, and this enables us to see how debts and indebtedness fit into this framework of understanding what it means to be human.

When we pray 'Our Father...' and ask him to 'forgive us our trespasses', we accept that we are not doing something individualistic. The prayer does not begin with the words 'My Father', but 'Our Father'. We acknowledge that being human under God involves our mutual obligations to our fellow humans, and that we cannot have the one (God as our Father) without the other (our obligations to others and theirs to us). The petition 'as we forgive them...' is our acknowledgement of this fact. It is not laying down conditions that God must fulfil; it is acknowledging that we have no automatic right to God's forgiveness, especially if our own behaviour wants to exempt us from what we mean when we pray 'Our Father...'.

I now want to move on to two passages which are very interesting, because their provenance in the New Testament textual tradition is disputed, one much more than the other, and to ask why this might be so.

On the Cross, Jesus asks God to forgive his executioners: 'Father, forgive them, for they know not what they do'. I looked through a number of translations and the only one of them that actually brought out the proper continuous force of the Greek word *elegen* was by J.B. Phillips. Although, in Greek, there are what we call 'aspects', there are languages, particularly Slavonic languages, Russian and Polish, that have 'aspects', signifying the different verbal forms that define whether an action is happening once, or whether it is a continual action. For example, in Polish, you use one particular verb if you say, 'I am going to the station – now', and a different verbal form if you mean, 'Every morning I go to the station'.

So this distinction that we call 'aspects', between an action that happens once and something that keeps on happening, is represented occasionally in Greek, and it is here; because *elegen* is the imperfect of *legei*, and it means Jesus said continuously. If he had said it once, it would have been *eipen*, 'Jesus said'. Oddly enough, only Phillips brings this out: Jesus *was saying*, 'Father, forgive them, for they know not what they do.' I think that is quite significant. It wasn't just once, although it was the First Word from the Cross; if we are to understand the Greek, Jesus kept on saying it as he was being nailed to the Cross. But it is not present in some important manuscripts, and therefore you may have a modern translation of the Bible that prints the verse, but may put some double lines on either side. I have a copy of the Greek New Testament where the verse is placed in brackets.

So we have to ask the question: Was this verse left out, accidentally or deliberately, or was it put in? A very strong case can be made for the view that the verse was left out, and it was left out because people found it offensive. Here is somebody being nailed to a cross, and what is he doing? He is saying, not once but continually, 'Father, forgive them, for they know not what they do'. How on earth can anybody do that? Another view is that although Jesus is not being crucified by Jews, but by Roman soldiers, there is this deep association in Christian thinking that the Jews were responsible for the death of Jesus; and so some people think that it was left out because it could be said to be taking the responsibility for doing this away from the Jews. But whatever it is, and we don't know for certain, I find the argument very persuasive that this verse very, very early on in the Greek New Testament copy in the manuscript tradition was offensive, and was therefore left out because it was so radical.

Then we come to the story whose textual evidence is even less firm than that of the First Word from the Cross: the story of the woman taken in adultery (John 7.53 - 8.11), which also occurs in Luke, within the Lucan Passion narrative (Luke 21:38-end). Interestingly, commentators point out that the language of the story is much closer to that of Luke than to that of John. You will remember how the story goes: a woman who has been caught in the act of adultery has been brought to Jesus for him to pronounce judgement on her, and of course there are all sorts of side issues here. Where is the *man*? How is it that the woman is discovered and not the man? After all, the Old Testament Law is quite clear: both are equally guilty. Has the woman been put up, has she been paid, in order to come along and be the object of this test for Jesus? But you'll remember what Jesus does; he says, 'Let him who is without sin among you be the first to throw a stone at her'. This goes back to the point, of course, that in cases of adultery such people are to be stoned to death. Stoning is rather a gruesome business of the person being put down into a pit with huge boulders being pushed down on to them, and it is the job of the witnesses to be the first people to push these boulders down. If ever you saw the film *The Life of Brian,* there is a very good enactment of that.

So the point is that Jesus does not condemn the woman; in the story he appears to forgive the woman and to say to her simply, 'Has no-one condemned you? Neither do I condemn you; go, and do not sin again'. Now, we are faced with the same problem. Why was it that this story seems to have floated around within the gospel tradition and finished up in a very few manuscripts in Luke and in a few more in John? Again it may well be the difficulty of coming to terms with a story like this, which appears to show an attitude of Jesus that goes quite against what people feel should be a moral administering of the law. So I think it is fascinating that we have these two passages, both of which seem to have had problems in the manuscript tradition.

Now we move on to where the presence of Jesus in the world inspires people to turn to him for help, sometimes involving forgiveness. In Mark 2.1-12 we have the story about the friends of the paralysed man, bringing him to Jesus and letting him down through the roof. The first thing that Jesus says is, 'My son, your sins are forgiven', and after that, he heals the man. This then starts off a controversy with the Jewish authorities there, who say that Jesus does not have the authority to forgive sins. The interesting thing in this case is that it is the faith of other people bringing this man to Jesus that elicits his response.

We now begin to move out of the Jewish embeddedness of the teaching of Jesus on forgiveness into something that is much more radical. I refer to the Parable of the Prodigal Son and the Elder Brother, because both are important in understanding this parable. In my Durham days I was asked to give a talk on the parables of Jesus in a part of Sunderland called East Herrington. I've never forgotten the fact that there was a woman present who was deeply upset by this parable, because her career and marriage had been affected by devoutly nursing her mother. She felt that it was grossly unfair that the elder brother, who had done all the good and right things, seems to be at a disadvantage when compared with the prodigal son.

Now, again, I have read sermons that try to rubbish the elder brother: 'He wouldn't have enjoyed a party, even if someone had given a party for him. He was a real spoilsport, he just got on with his work.' We mustn't do that. We have to allow full credit to the elder brother for staying at home, by doing his work, by contributing to the family income and the family farm. We have to make full allowance for that; and then to see in the father's treatment of the prodigal a sort of radicality that tells us about the morality of grace which is active in the ministry of Jesus, because the action of the father in the parable takes place within a relationship: 'This my son was dead, and is alive; he was lost, and is found'.

It may seem to go against all our normal ideas of loyalty, reward, whatever, that the father should see the son from afar off, should run to meet him, should order all these celebrations, and say, 'This my son was dead, and is alive; he was lost, and is found'. And yet this is what the morality of grace is about, and it runs so contrary to what we rightly think is good responsible behaviour that we would all want to emulate, looking after elderly people, caring for others, and so on. And so, if we cannot understand this parable, it is precisely because there is active here a morality of grace with radical implications for the world in which we normally live.

We are beginning to get a glimpse here, I think, of what is going to happen when we arrive at a Christian idea of the forgiveness of sins, and confront the world of normal, proper relationships with that morality of grace.

When we come to the Parable of the Pharisee and the Publican (Luke 18.9-14) we have something rather similar. Again, I have heard sermons and read sermons in which the Pharisee is rubbished – he was a hypocrite, he prayed with himself, as it says in the story – and we feel we really have to rubbish him. No, we mustn't rubbish him! If we wanted to invite either of these two people to a party, it would have been the Pharisee we would have invited, not the publican. The Pharisee was a decent, honest, upright man, even if he was a bit self-confident and self-boasting about himself. It is the publican, the tax collector, the man who dared not lift up his eyes unto heaven who goes down justified. I came across a fascinating comment on this in T.W. Manson,[22] who says that there is a paradox here: the publican confesses that he is guilty, and yet he is the one who goes down to his house justified. Notice that word 'justified', because although it is a complicated perfect participle, it comes from that same *dikaios* root in Greek that is all about being righteous and justified. This man went down to his house justified rather than the other. We have again this radical view of things that, within the relationship that God has with his people, forgiveness works in rather odd ways.

Finally we come to the Parables of the Lost Sheep and the Lost Coin (Luke 18.4-10). Again, there is something odd, certainly in the parable of the shepherd, who, having lost one sheep leaves the ninety-nine, and goes to look for it. This is irrational behaviour, because who is going to look after the ninety-nine

---

[22] T. W. Manson, *The Sayings of Jesus as Recorded in the Gospels according to St Matthew and St Luke*, London: SCM Press, 1950.

sheep? The ninety-nine sheep are going to be left defenceless. Robbers, wolves, may come and devastate the flock. This makes no sense at all; he's still got ninety-nine sheep, so why is he bothering about one?

The remarkable thing about both of these parables is that they afford us a 'glimpse' into what it costs God to forgive and the 'absurdity' of divine grace (I've put the word 'glimpse' in inverted commas, because when we are talking about God's feelings, we can only do this through imperfect human language, and we mustn't project our feelings and emotions on to God). But as I have said before in sermons at the Abbey – and this goes back to a marvellous book by Oliver Quick – that our own experience of losing something enables us to understand these parables.[23] We have all lost something at some time in our life, and even if it was a very unimportant trivial thing, we have felt a sense of incompleteness, a sense of incompleteness out of all proportion to the fact that we haven't lost 99.99% of the rest of our possessions! We look for the pen or the thing or whatever it is, we look for it, and when we find it, we have a satisfaction and joy that is out of all proportion to how insignificant this lost object is, and certainly in relation to all the things we haven't lost at all. As the parable says, 'There will be more joy in heaven over one sinner who repents than over ninety-nine righteous persons who need no repentance'. This interesting tie-up with human experience of losing things perhaps gives us some sense of what is going on in the whole business of the radicality of the morality of grace.

Now, one thing I haven't mentioned is the penitent thief on the cross. A big question that keeps coming up with regard to forgiveness is, 'What does penitence mean?' Of course we are

---

[23] Oliver Quick, *The Realism of Christ's Parables*, London: SCM Press, 1952

used to saying in our liturgies, 'Make us sorry for our sins', or we say that 'we are sorry for our sins'. I don't see in any of these incidents that I have spoken about that feeling sorry is necessarily a factor in all this. It is rather that Jesus forgives the penitent thief, whose penitence does not involve feeling sorry, so much as recognising who Jesus is. Strictly speaking, of course, to repent, taking it back to its Jewish origins *shuv*, means 'to turn'. It is not about feelings; it is about changing course. In the case of the Old Testament it is about altering course back to God within the context of the special relationship. In the case of Jesus' dealing with people, it is to recognise that in Jesus there is hope, whereas elsewhere there is no hope to be found. That is certainly what the thief on the cross seems to perceive.

So we are finding ourselves, then, within the context of the special relationship, and now have been given an edge by this radical outworking of what I call 'the morality of grace'. The one element of truth in theories about God not being able to forgive unless some price, some sacrifice, is paid, is that divine forgiveness is costly. But it is not costly in the way that we think it is; it is costly in a different way. We are approaching Holy Week and Good Friday, when we shall think about the Passion of Jesus. But in the Passion of Jesus, I would argue, Jesus does not suffer the wrath of God, which is the necessary condition for God to be able to forgive. What Jesus does is that he confronts the wickedness of a world and a human race under the domination of evil. And by entering into confrontation with evil and sin in this way, he robs them of their power to have the last word.

When we come on to think about Paul in the next lecture, we shall see that the most common understanding that Paul has of the meaning of the death of Christ is that it confronts and defeats what he calls 'the principalities and the powers' who, for once, overstep themselves, who think that they are going to have the last word, and discover the enormous mistake that they have made. So we move away from the idea of the courtroom. We move into the sphere of financial indebtedness, and that then begins to make so much more sense of the Bible and hopefully of ourselves.

CHAPTER 4

Sin and Forgiveness in the Teaching of Paul

I feel somewhat diffident about giving a lecture on Paul, because the study of Paul is a tremendously specialist and complex thing, and I am a mere Old Testament specialist, though I've also taught courses in my Durham days on the Dead Sea Scrolls and Intertestamental Judaism. So it is with some trepidation that I address myself to Paul; but perhaps I can give you a little bit of autobiography here, so that you can see where I am coming from. I came into Christian faith through the teaching of Jesus, particularly the Parables of the Kingdom of God, and it took me some while to come to terms with Paul. I think this was partly because of unhelpful ways that people spoke, and even wrote, about Paul, and my engagement with Paul has been a long journey. It has been a very rewarding journey, because the more I have studied Paul, and I've done it a great deal, I have come to appreciate Paul for my own Christian faith, and to see what a debt we owe to him as an interpreter and preacher of the Gospel. So, that's my autobiography, and explains how and why I am coming to Paul, very much more from an Old Testament background, whereas I think Pauline specialists tend to do it more from a Graeco-Roman background.

Well, it is no surprise that Paul, having spent the first part of his adult life, perhaps most of his adult life, as a Pharisee and an observant Jew, one who had studied in Jerusalem, it is no surprise that he is rooted in the Old Testament and in that special relationship that I was talking about when we dealt with the Old Testament. So it is no surprise that in Romans he quotes from Psalm 32:

> Blessed is he whose transgression is forgiven, whose sin is covered. Blessed is the man unto whom the Lord imputeth not iniquity, and in whose spirit there is no guile. (vv.1-2)

But, for Paul, God, through the death and resurrection of Jesus, has created a new special relationship, and it has universal and cosmic implications. For these latter, I am referring to Romans 8:22, that enigmatic passage where Paul talks about the creation 'groaning in travail' and being in bondage, and looking forward to the revealing of the sons of God. Alas, he doesn't elaborate on that, though from an Old Testament point of view, one cannot help thinking of those great passages in Isaiah 11 and Isaiah 65 that envisage a new heaven and a new earth, where we get the vegetarian lion, a creation freed from the violence that inhabits it:

> They shall not hurt nor destroy in all my holy mountain, saith the Lord' (Isaiah 65.25)

We shall see later on, of course, that Paul has this tremendous sense that the things that will happen at the end of the age are happening now; and if, at the end of the age, the creation is to be renewed, then there is a sense in which that can or should be happening now. Paul has various phrases for this new dimension of grace; so Colossians 1.13:

> God hath delivered us from the power of darkness, and hath translated us into the kingdom of his dear Son,

and he speaks on more than one occasion about the Kingdom. And then in Galatians:

> There is neither Jew nor Greek, there is neither bond nor free, there is neither male nor female, for ye are all one in Christ Jesus (3.28)

'Being in Christ Jesus' is another of the phrases that he uses for this new special relationship that God has created. But the importance of this for the forgiveness of sins is not that God has now made these Old Testament facilities available universally, but that God's forgiveness operates universally in a *new dimension*, a new dimension created by God through Jesus Christ, a dimension that stands over and against the normal world. This is the significance of Galatians 3.28, that 'there is neither Jew nor Greek, there is neither bond nor free, there is neither male nor female'.

Within this new special relationship, you have human relationships that stand, as opposed to what was normal in the world at the time. In II Corinthians 5.17, we have the words:

> Therefore if any man be in Christ, he is a new creature: old things are passed away; behold, all things are become new.

We are talking about a new special relationship, a new dimension of grace that is universal and cosmic in its implications, but that stands opposed to what we might call the normal, unredeemed world; and this has all come about because of this very difficult concept of the 'righteousness of God'.

Now, in Greek and also in Hebrew, these words 'righteousness',' just', 'justified', 'to justify', all centre in the Greek around this verbal stem of *dík*, and of course in Hebrew, similarly, you get a connection between *tsadaq* and *tsedaqah*, meaning 'to justify', 'righteousness', and so on. Now, God's righteousness is not what God *is*; God's righteousness is what he *does*. It is the exercise of his sovereignty in putting things and people right. There is a lovely quotation from T. W. Manson's book, *On Paul and John*, where he says, 'God acts not as administrator of the law, but as king in his own kingdom, and father of his own children'.[24] This righteousness has been achieved in and through Christ, and thus this important passage, II Corinthians 5.19:

> God was in Christ, reconciling the world unto himself, not imputing their trespasses unto them –

and he goes on to talk about the ministry of reconciliation with which he has been entrusted. We begin to see in Paul's teaching here that element of absurdity that we noticed in the last lecture in the teaching of Jesus. You will remember that I was talking about the Parable of the Prodigal Son, and how this parable could upset people who feel that all the loyal service of the elder brother was brushed aside, was all for nothing, and that the treatment by the father of the prodigal was really scandalous. This young man has wasted his substance in riotous living and comes crawling back, this disreputable creature; and yet the father is looking out for him, and runs to him, embraces him, orders the robe, and all this to be done for him; there is this element of absurdity. This element of absurdity also comes through in the teaching of Paul: that what God has done in Jesus in setting up this new special relationship defies normal logic:

> But we preach Christ crucified, unto the Jews a stumbling block, and unto the Greeks foolishness; but unto them which are called, both Jews and Greeks, Christ the power

---

[24] T. W. Manson, *On Paul and John. Some Selected Theological Themes.* Studies in Biblical Theology No 38, London: SCM Press, 1963.

of God, and the wisdom of God. Because the foolishness of God is wiser than men; and the weakness of God is stronger than men (I Corinthians 1.23-5)

This is a lesson that the Church is very reluctant to learn, that the foolishness of God is wiser than men; because one of the difficulties about this whole subject, the Atonement, forgiveness, is the refusal of the Church to acknowledge that the foolishness of God is wiser than men, and the desire of the Church to hold God accountable to *our* ideas of justice and forgiveness and so on. The foolishness of God is wiser than men means that we have to let God be God, and what he does defies normal logic:

> For when we were yet without strength, in due time Christ died for the ungodly. For scarcely for a righteous man will one die: yet peradventure for a good man some would even dare to die. But God commendeth his love toward us, in that, while we were yet sinners, Christ died for us. (Romans 5.6-8)

So we come to this phrase, 'justification by faith'. What is it? I would say that justification by faith is the discovery and acknowledgement by individuals that Christ died for the ungodly, that is, for *them*. Compare this with Galatians 2.20, a verse I shall come back to later on:

> The life which I now live in the flesh I live by the faith of the Son of God, who loved me, and gave himself for me. (Galatians 2.20)

That is a declaration of justification by faith: the discovery that the Son of God loved me and gave himself for me, and the transforming effect that that realisation and that discovery can have upon the life of individuals and communities.

Christ's death and resurrection have implications for law, and for the Law. Paul does not believe in an amoral universe. He knows the good news that God is coming to judge the world; and so we have, in Psalm 98, the joyous acclamation:

> Let the sea roar, and the fullness thereof; the world, and they that dwell therein. Let the floods clap their hands: let the hills be joyful together before the Lord; for he cometh to judge the earth: with righteousness shall he judge the world, and the people with equity. (Psalm 98.7-9)

Judgement is part of the good news; part of the good news, because I don't want to live in a world where it doesn't matter whether you're Adolf Hitler or Mother Teresa (whatever you might say about Mother Teresa). I don't want to live in that sort of world, a world that is totally indifferent morally. The idea that God will judge is good news. Paul says that we must appear before the judgement seat of Christ, and he speaks of God's wrath in Romans 1.18. We hear this idea, the wrath of God, and say, 'Oh dear, oh dear, this is the Old Testament God of wrath! We don't want that, we want the New Testament God of love!' And yet, whether or not the words 'wrath', or 'anger' are appropriate, I would somehow feel let down if I thought that God was indifferent to the many things in the world that make me angry. I am angry at the way in which the wealth of this world is so unjustly distributed. I am angry at the way in which we are devastating the created order with which we have been entrusted. I am angry that women and children are abused. I don't have to go on; I am sure you can add to the list and you can say, 'Yes, we are angry, rightly angry, about these things. We don't want to live in a world where these things are going to have the last word.'

The assurance that we have in the Old Testament, which speaks of God coming to judge the world, of our having to appear before the judgement seat of Christ, however we understand that, and Paul speaking about God's wrath against wickedness, all this is right. It is God's judgement against lawlessness in a world where men 'worshipped and served the creature more than the Creator' (Romans 1.25). And law is necessary; we cannot have an ordered society without it, and our politicians are constantly talking about the rule of law. But we have to take one step beyond that. Law and the Jewish Law have their limitations. Paul would have been aware, I would have thought, of the teaching of one of the great Jewish teachers, Simeon the Just. We do not know exactly who he was – he might have been the High Priest around 280, he might have been a later descendant, perhaps around 200 – but in that most important document of Jewish ethics, *The Sayings of the Jewish Fathers* (*Pirke Aboth*), we have this extremely important statement:

> Upon three things the world stands [i.e., there are three things of fundamental importance]: the Law [the Torah], worship and [a marvellous phrase, difficult to translate], the imparting of kindnesses.[25]

And so in addition to the law, you have worship. The importance of worship is that we ascribe the glory to God, and we realise our littleness in relation to him. And then the imparting of kindnesses covers that area of life where law cannot have any place at all: those acts of generosity, of goodwill, visiting the sick, doing all those things that cannot be prescribed by law. One of the things that has been so tragic in the recent history of our country is the way in which so many things, such as teaching and the health service, used to run on the imparting of kindnesses. People used to run classes after school, used to take children on school trips, and then suddenly along comes a politician and says, 'No, you've got to have a contract, it's got to be regulated by law.' And all of a sudden those acts of kindness get snuffed out, because if

---

[25] *Pirke Aboth*, 1.2. Author's own translation from the traditional text.

people are going to be treated as though they have to be stuck to the law, then they will. This sense of the imparting of kindnesses is a very important thing, and this is a very profound insight within the Judaism that Paul, I think, knew or should have known. But Paul then goes further, which is so interesting:

> For if there had been a law given which could have given life, verily righteousness should have been by the law. (Galatians 3.21)

Because, for the Early Christians looking at the death of Christ, law and sin showed their limitations by crucifying Christ. When we read the Passion on Good Friday, we see this at work, we see how people do things against their better judgement; and there is an air of hypocrisy, of unreality, which then leads to the convenience of crucifying Christ, and brings with it, in the process, that innate brutality in human nature, which, when it gets the chance to victimise and bully, will do so.

And so the death of Christ exposes the weakness of the law and it also defeated the people that Paul calls 'the princes of this world'. Now, I shall come on to those a little later on, but this is a very important part of Paul's teaching. Closely allied to Paul's teaching about the limitations of law and the Jewish Law, there is an important distinction between the letter and the spirit: 'The letter killeth, but the spirit giveth life' (II Corinthians 3.6). Here we see a link from Paul back to the ministry of Jesus, because we see in the ministry of Jesus in the Gospels this same conflict: Jesus is accused of being a law-breaker; his disciples pluck ears of corn on the Sabbath; Jesus heals people on the Sabbath, and so on. He lays down the idea that the Sabbath law has its limitations: 'The Sabbath was made for man, and not man for the Sabbath' (Mark 2.27). In his teaching about the Holy Spirit and the fruits of the Spirit in Galatians 5.22, Paul lists all these things: love, joy, peace, long-suffering, self-control; against these, he says significantly, there is no law.

So this is the first problem with the law. Although law is necessary, although judgement is something to be welcomed, there is another dimension also – the Holy Spirit. This governs that part of life which appeals to our generosity, and, indeed, appeals to the Biblical point of view in responding to what I call 'the imperatives of redemption', which I was talking about with regard to the Old Testament. The law, in league with sin, human vulnerability, and principalities and powers, has imprisoned and enslaved the human race. These principalities and powers are hinted at darkly in Romans 8.38; they are not mentioned together there, but Paul says that the love of God cannot separate us from principalities *or* powers, and references to these also occur elsewhere.

We can understand that against the background of what we find in the Dead Sea Scrolls. There, the writers of the community rule speak of 'the angel of darkness'. The people of the covenant community, who are called 'the children of light', find themselves ranged against 'the children of darkness'. The children of darkness are controlled by what the covenant has called 'the angel of darkness'. But the angel of darkness also interferes in the activities of the children of light, and there is one passage that ascribes all their weaknesses and failings to the action of the angel of darkness. I think Paul also realises that, in addition to powers of darkness, there are all the structural things that govern human life, which can also imprison humans and stop them from doing and being what they want to do or be.

There has been a lot of recent writing about this – an American scholar, Walter Wink, has done some work on it – but whether or not it is convincing is another matter entirely. I think, from our point of view, that we are not necessarily bound to believe in powers of darkness, or a personal devil, or whatever, except that it seems that the reality is this: that weakness and sin are such that they draw their strength from us; they draw their strength from the wrong choices that we make. This is what Genesis 4 is all about, the story of Cain and Abel. Cain makes this decision and is told that 'sin is crouching at the door; its desire is for you' (v.7). When we try to do good things – try to defend people who are being threatened by dictators, and so on – as soon as we open the door, somehow the wickedness in some seemingly organised, semi-personal way seems to come in to take control, and suddenly it is beyond our control. The important thing is not so much how we think of it conceptually, but that we recognise the reality. This then brings me on to that astonishing passage in Romans 7, which has caused so much controversy and disagreement:

> For I know that in me (that is in my flesh,) dwelleth no good thing: for to will is present with me; but how to perform that which is good I find not. For the good that I would I do not: but the evil which I would not, that I do. Now if I do that I would not, it is no more I that do it, but sin that dwelleth in me. I find then a law, that, when I would do good, evil is present with me. For I delight in the law of God after the inward man: but I see another law in my members, warring against the law of my mind, and bringing me into captivity to the law of sin, which is in my members. O wretched man that I am! who shall deliver me from the body of this death? I thank God through Jesus Christ our Lord. (Romans 7.18-25)

This has generated an enormous amount of discussion, especially if it is seen simply personally. Is this Paul speaking before he became a Christian, or is it Paul speaking after he became a Christian? If we have to choose between these alternatives, I would say that he is describing his situation after he becomes a Christian. But one can take this in a wider sense, and I want to take this in a wider sense, in terms of the general frustrations for Christians, indeed, for sensitive and religious people, in an imperfect world.

On the occasion when I preached here on the fiftieth anniversary of my ordination, I said that in my first few weeks of being ordained, I realised that if I wanted to do all the things that were necessary to be done, I would kill myself in a matter of months! You begin with this sense of 'the conversion of the world in our generation', and then you begin to realise your own weakness, your own limitations, the limitations of the systems with which we have to work. I wonder how many people there are who want to do good things, and yet in the world organised as it is, they cannot necessarily achieve them. Indeed, the consequences of doing good may sometimes be bad, and the other way round. I think that these words in Romans 7, however they may have described some of Paul's inner turmoil, also describe our dilemma in the world in which we live, a world in which we want to do good, and yet very often we cannot do it.

It is a world also in which sometimes we cannot avoid doing what we do not want to do; we sometimes find ourselves confronted with choices where we have to choose the lesser evil, when we would not want to do either of these evils. And so there is something tremendously paradoxical here in expressing the tensions that will arise if we are concerned to try to be true to what God has done in Jesus Christ, and to live and apply these things in the world around us. There is a sense, therefore, in which sin and lawlessness, for all that the law is important, has us imprisoned; and we might cry out with Paul, 'How are we going to get out of this?' And we will have to say, somehow, 'I thank God, through Jesus Christ'.

And so we come to this whole business of what we might call the 'eschatology'. I mentioned it right at the beginning, when I said that Paul's vision of the world of the created order in travail, waiting for release, takes me back to Isaiah 11 and Isaiah 65, these things that could happen at the end of the age. In Old Testament thinking, the Holy Spirit is the gift of the age to come; but for Paul and his followers, the age to come has now come, even within the limitations of a world not fully redeemed. This is consonant, of course, with the preaching of Jesus: 'The time is fulfilled, and the kingdom of God is at hand' (Mark 1.15). The kingdom is operating in the ministry of Jesus, and people are being invited to enter into that kingdom of right relationships. Because of this, there is a dialectical tension in Paul between the present and the future; and the forgiveness of sins within this new cosmic special relationship is one that sets up conflict with a world still dominated by law, sin, principalities and powers, and disregard of God.

This is what I'm going to have to try to pull together in the next lecture, when I try to see how the Christian view of the forgiveness of sins within its proper Christian setting has to confront and talk to a world which has taken the words 'forgiveness' and 'sins' and used them in their own way, and we have to see how we confront them. One of the ways in which we confront them is by the proclamation of the Gospel. The proclamation of the Gospel is not an offer of success within the limitations of a world not fully redeemed; it is a challenge to the very foundations of that world. Hearing and following the Gospel leads to conflict and suffering, and those are well illustrated in Paul's life and ministry and by the dialectical nature of his utterances. Here are three examples:

> But by the grace of God I am what I am ... but I laboured more abundantly than they all: yet not I, but the grace of God which was with me. (I Corinthians 15.10)
>
> By honour and dishonour, by evil report and good report: as deceivers, and yet true; as unknown, and yet well known; as dying, and, behold, we live; as chastened, and not killed; as sorrowful, yet alway rejoicing; as poor, yet making many rich; as having nothing, and yet possessing all things. (II Corinthians 6.8-10)
>
> I am crucified with Christ; nevertheless I live; yet not I, but Christ liveth in me: and the life which I now live in the flesh I live by the faith of the Son of God, who loved me, and gave himself for me. (Galatians 2.20)

So we are beginning to see, I hope, that in Paul as I understand him, the forgiveness of sins operates within this new special dimension of grace which God has created though Jesus Christ. It is a dimension of grace that contains the spirit rather than the letter, the absurdity of a God who justifies the ungodly; and yet it is this reality that has to confront the world, for people to be invited into this reality, to see life in terms of this reality.

Paul expected the imminent return of Jesus, as did the first generations of Christians. As the expectation of this *Parousia*, this Appearing, receded, Christian thought accommodated itself to a one-dimensional, non-eschatological view of reality, in which it is the *Church* that occupies the place of the special relationship, and now provides a system of forgiveness, designed mainly to ensure entry into the world to come. That this was a betrayal of the teaching of Paul and Jesus, is indicated by the various radical movements in Christianity that have arisen from time to time, movements that have not been content with this idea that we live in a one-dimensional world, where somehow the Gospel is fitted into the normal state of affairs. In its most bizarre form, we have the 'prosperity gospel' in some parts of the world, where to be a Christian is a way to acquire material blessing within the terms of this world – an awful distortion, it seems to me, of the teaching of Jesus and Paul. We have had various things, such as the monastic movement, the attempt to live alternative lifestyles. Our Abbey here is connected with that, and we may think that some of the manifestations were bizarre, such as people sitting at the top of pillars to be on their own. Or we think of the various charismatic movements, beginning in the Early Church with the Montanists and the prophetesses. In our own days, one of the attractions of the charismatic movement, whatever we may think of it, is that there are people talking about energies that challenge what normally goes on in the world, the gifts of the Spirit, an emphasis that something is happening, or should be happening, that points forwards to the consummation.

At the end of this, my journey into Paul, I now have to ask myself how I can take these insights from Paul and Jesus and articulate a Christian view of the forgiveness of sins that will come into dialogue, challenging dialogue, with a world that does not understand the Christian use of these terms, a world which has its own uses of these terms, but a world that desperately needs to hear and to know the Christian uses and understanding of these terms?

CHAPTER 5

The Forgiveness of Sinners in Today's World

I have a confession to make. It is this: as I prepared this final lecture, I have been wondering whether I have been lecturing on the wrong subject; that I shouldn't have been speaking about the forgiveness of *sins*, but about the forgiveness of *sinners*. And if I could change one word in the Apostles' Creed (which of course I can't), I would make it finish in the following way:

> I believe in the Holy Ghost; the Holy Catholick Church; the Communion of Saints; the Forgiveness of *Sinners*; the Resurrection of the body, and the Life everlasting. Amen.

What is the difference between talking about the forgiveness of *sins* and the forgiveness of *sinners*? Sins are things – things done, things thought, things said, things not done – and it is possible for us to separate off these things from ourselves. After all, most of us middle-class professional people living in Britain live fairly decent, upright, commendable lives. We have these moments when we say, or think, or do things that we shouldn't have done, but these are only small things; and when we come to church on a Sunday, we can separate those things from ourselves, we can lay them before God, we can hope that God can somehow deal with them, wipe the slate clean, give us a fresh start, so that we can go back to our usual, normal, fairly decent, honest lives. If we talk about the forgiveness of *sinners*, we are not talking about sins as things; we are talking, first of all, about a relationship, a relationship with God, a relationship that God has created, and has created in such a way that sins are not so much what we *do*, but sins are what we *are* – or rather *sinners* is what we are.

Now, how does that come about? It comes about, first of all, through God's almighty 'Yes!' to us in Jesus Christ. I've mentioned before in Beauchief Abbey the old Persil advertisement, where somebody is wearing a nice, clean, white shirt. Someone comes and stands next to him, wearing a shirt washed in Persil, and immediately you see the difference between the nice, white shirt and the Persil-washed shirt that makes the nice, white shirt look rather grubby by comparison. In Isaiah 64.6, you get the same: 'All our righteousnesses are as filthy rags'. Perhaps that's a little bit of an exaggeration, but you'll see what I mean. Because God's 'Yes!' to us in Jesus Christ, God's coming to us in Jesus Christ, shows us what a life of true love, of true sacrifice, of true self-giving is; and, by comparison, we begin to realise that however decent our lives may be, they fall short of the glory of God in the sense of Christ's coming. But Christ doesn't come in order to show us up; he comes to invite us into his kingdom, he comes to show us his grace. And, remembering what I was saying before about sin, and the law, and all the structural wrongness that there is in the world, the things that imprison us and ensnare us, Christ comes also to deliver us from sin in that respect. One of the great insights of Luther and Lutheranism is that we are at one and the same time justified and sinners. So that when we come to think about forgiveness, forgiveness is not just a matter of dealing with bits and pieces that we have done. To want God's forgiveness is to feel that we have let down somebody who has been gracious towards us, we have betrayed a trust; we are in a relationship and we have not been true to that relationship. And so, when in that context we say that we are sorry, we are not doing what we have learned to do since we were little children, to use the word 'sorry' as a sort of truce word that wards off the annoyance of the parent. We are not trying to simulate or manufacture false feelings of guilt in the hope that God will look favourably upon us because we are feeling sorry. Within the context of the forgiveness of sinners, to feel sorry is to be really sorry that we have let down someone to whom we owe so much. So I think that there is a very big difference between talking about the forgiveness of sins and the forgiveness of sinners.

I was warning at the end of the previous lecture about falling into that one-dimensional attitude which emerged in the history of the Church. You'll remember that I was speaking about the excitement that we have in the New Testament that 'the age to come' has come, the kingdom is present in Jesus, and people are invited to enter that kingdom, that sphere of God's rule. And you'll remember that I was saying that in Jewish apocalyptic, the Holy Spirit is the gift at the end of the age. In the teaching of Paul, the Holy Spirit is now given; and those things that properly belong to the end-time are now part of our present, in dialectical tension with our present. I also said how the Church had lost this excitement of living in a world that was radically questioned by another dimension that God has established through Jesus Christ; and that we have become one-dimensional, with the Church merely being there as some sort of device for getting rid of our wrongdoings and sins. If we think in terms of the forgiveness of sinners, not the forgiveness of sins, then we emphasise that we are talking about a relationship which God has made possible. Because

God has made this possible, it is within the context of this special relationship, the context of his kingdom that is present with us; and in that way, we can perhaps avoid falling into that one-dimensionalism that I think is a curse of so much.

And so I will continue to talk about holding on tenaciously to these ideas that express the special character of the relationship which God in his grace and mercy has established with us. This means that we must think about the justification of the ungodly, and that we are the ungodly – not in any radical, sinning sense, but in the way in which God coming to us shows us the need of grace in comparison with him. In other words, we have to talk about the foolishness of God, to talk about the weakness of God, to talk about the dimension of the Spirit. It is no surprise that in the history of the Church from time to time there have been movements, beginning with the Montanists in the Early Church in the second century, who wanted to emphasise, perhaps over-emphasise, the Spirit and the gifts of the Spirit. It is no surprise that charismatic churches should have a certain amount of attractiveness to people, as they seem to portray something different from the normal, one-dimensional routine of the Church. And in mentioning here the dimension of *agape*, I want to remind you of I Corinthians 13. I always think there is an inspired translation of this in Moffatt's New Testament, where again we have a description of this special dimension, created by God, in terms of love. As my dear friend and colleague from Durham days, Charles Kingsley Barrett, used to say, this is a portrait of Christ:

> Love is very patient, very kind. Love knows no jealousy; love makes no parade, gives itself no airs, is never rude, never selfish, never irritated, never resentful; love is never glad when others go wrong, love is gladdened by goodness, always slow to expose, always eager to believe the best, always hopeful, always patient. Love never

disappears. As for prophesying, it will be superseded; as for 'tongues,' they will cease; as for knowledge, it will be superseded. (I Corinthians 13.4-8)

As we read that amazing description of love in I Corinthians 13 we are again apprised of that dimension and have a sense of how far short of it we fall – and yet we can only know of this through God's grace.

Now, because Christians must forgive their enemies, there are real problems when Christians do this in a non-Christian setting. Again, the words of Jesus are very uncompromising here:

> Ye have heard that it hath been said, Thou shalt love thy neighbour, and hate thine enemy. But I say unto you, Love your enemies, bless them that curse you, do good to them that hate you, and pray for them which despitefully use you, and persecute you; that ye may be the children of your Father which is in heaven: for he maketh his sun to rise on the evil and on the good, and sendeth rain on the just and on the unjust. For if ye love them which love you, what reward have ye? do not even the publicans the same? And if ye salute your brethren only, what do ye more than others? do not even the publicans so? Be ye therefore perfect, even as your Father which is in heaven is perfect. (Matthew 5:43-8)

Of course this is an unachievable aim, but a reminder in radical words that the one condition (as we learned in a previous lecture) that Jesus lays down for being forgiven by God is our readiness to forgive others. So it is not surprising that when non-Christians come upon Christian forgiveness, they find it difficult or impossible to understand what is going on. I was reminded of the fact that in October 2006, in the United States, in the county of Lincoln in Pennsylvania, a gunman went into an Amish school and shot dead ten small children. Now, you'll remember that the Amish are a rather unusual Christian manifestation; descended from Swiss and South German Protestants, they still use a form of German for some of their worship and even for some of their conversation, and eschew many of the alleged benefits of civilisation. They are a very close-knit, perhaps very authoritarian 'sect', as we might say. But the outcome of that shooting of ten small children was that they forgave the man who did it straightaway. This was quite incomprehensible, as you can imagine, to the reporters and the people who had gone there to report this atrocity: 'How can you forgive? What does it mean?' And so it should be no surprise to us that when Christians take the command of Christ into the world it is going to puzzle people, and it is right that it should puzzle people, because Christians are not coming from any position of superiority, and certainly not because they are better. Christians are coming from the point where they obey the command of Christ, and where they are seeking, no doubt with many failures and difficulties, to live in the dimension of grace and love and forgiveness which God has created.

But Christians have to live in the world. They are embedded in what A.D. Lindsay calls, in *The Two Moralities*, a marvellous book that I shall quote from later on, 'the morality of my station and its duties'.[26] As Christians, we have to take seriously the need to support and uphold the moral codes that enable life to go on harmoniously, so that we realise our reciprocal obligations, and we need to contribute to those. And we need to respect the law, notwithstanding the defects in the law pointed out by Paul, as we heard in last week's lecture, that the law cannot *command* people to love, the law cannot *command* people to do what the Jews called these 'acts of kindness'. But Christians have a contribution to make to

---

[26] A. D. Lindsay, *The Two Moralities: Our Duty to God and to Society*, London: Eyre and Spottiswoode, 1940.

secular discourse about law and order and wrongdoing and so on. We only have to remember how Christians such as Bishop Desmond Tutu in South Africa and the former Bishop of Liverpool in the Hillsborough Enquiry could make a contribution to discussions where people will have to be held to account. We cannot live in an immoral universe, where it doesn't matter whether you are Adolf Hitler or Mother Teresa; there must be an accounting. Judgement is good news, not bad news from a Christian point of view, and we have to go along with all that. The decision in the High Court recently *not* to release a former cab driver, convicted of sex and drug offences and whose release was causing so much anxiety, must be welcomed, because society has a right to protect its members in proper ways. So we have to be involved with all that, constructively, and help where we can, because Christians are often trusted in the judgements and the impartiality that they bring where these matters are being discussed. But we mustn't allow the *secular* discourse about forgiveness to corrupt our Christian discourse about the forgiveness of sinners. We have the famous saying, 'I will forgive, but I won't forget', and within a secular environment, that is quite a reasonable position to take. Whether or not it is a Christian view, I do not know. I do not think there is anything about these things in what Jesus says. I don't think Jesus mentioned this, but obviously we have these problems and we must not allow the secular language to influence our Christian language, because the only way in which we can help the world in which we live is by being absolutely clear about our position as Christians.

And so I have been thinking about Christian worship, which I am responsible for conducting on a regular basis, and I believe that we need to think, and perhaps teach, our congregations about how our Christian worship must reflect the special relationship which has called it into being. I once met a man who very sincerely said to me that his church was his club, which was fair enough – he went there, he met people there – but that was it, his church was his club. Well, perhaps, for us, I hope, the church is there because it is God's church, built upon the foundation of Jesus Christ and the prophets and the apostles, and so we must try to reflect this special relationship. I think we must begin with the Christian Liturgical Year, that ordering of time by which we shape our lives as Christians in a world that is trying to get rid of any idea of a Christian Liturgical Year. There used to be something called 'Whitsun'; that was abolished in favour of the 'Spring Bank Holiday'. Christmas in some circles is called 'Yuletide', and when it comes to Easter, the symbol of Easter is not a Cross or an empty tomb, but an Easter bunny on many of the cards we see in the shops. And so we must resist this idea. When I lived in Durham, I used to help out at a church called St Paul's, Spennymoor, and I used to travel on the Bishop Auckland bus from Durham to Spennymoor. There was one particular part I used to go through – I'm talking about over forty years ago – and in all the windows of the houses there were little notices saying, 'This is Holy Week', and then on Easter Sunday the bottom of it would be unfolded to reveal the words, 'He is risen today'. But it was a reminder. County Durham was in some ways rather behind what I'd been used to, but all the shops were closed in those days in many parts of County Durham on Good Friday. I don't know whether shops were ever closed here on Good Friday – Sheffield has a very secular history, and there it is. But we need to remember and emphasise the Christian Liturgical Year: we think in terms of the year based upon the life of Christ, because the life and death and resurrection of Christ are what it is all about. As I was saying in the very first lecture, the phrase 'the forgiveness of sins' (or, as I would change it, 'the forgiveness of sinners') comes in the Creed, the Creed which is centred upon Jesus

Christ. And, secondly, the Eucharist is the visible expression of, and thanksgiving for, the justification of the ungodly.

In the 1950s, '60s and '70s, there was something called the Liturgical Movement, which did a lot of good things, actually, and yet sometimes there was an emphasis on the Eucharist that was anything but to do with the justification of the ungodly. In fact, I think people would have felt it was rather offensive to talk about the justification of the ungodly as centred in the Eucharist. There was this idea that it was all about Creation, that we came to God, that the bread and wine represented the things of human life, the work of our hands, and we offer them to God, who offers them back to us, and this completely disregarded the Eucharist being in any way connected with the Passover, which is of course a slightly problematic thing. But in the Passover, certainly, the bread and the wine used in the Passover were *symbols* of the oppression of the Israelites and God's freeing of the Israelites from that oppression. I think, therefore, without making the Eucharist in any way gloomy, and remembering that 'Eucharist' means 'thanksgiving', we want to make the Eucharist the thanksgiving for the fact that the ungodly are justified. After all, what is the central thing in the Book of Common Prayer? It is Jesus' coming; and so we give thanks for the one oblation of himself once offered, the sacrifice for the sins of the whole world. It is centred on that, and as we come to the Communion Table, we come as sinners. We come as sinners in that special relationship which God has created. But what we have done, what we are apart from being sinners, is all forgotten. There is only one thing that we are – whether male, female, bond, free, Greek, Jew – and that is those who are invited by God to come to his table, to receive those visible symbols of his love, acceptance, forgiveness and grace.

And then, when we come to the Intercessions in our service, again we have to remember that interceding is something that does not go on, usually, in secular institutions. It is something rather special about the Church that we pray for the Queen and the government and those in authority over us, and so on. We have to remember, therefore, that when we do the intercessions, we are making a distinctive contribution to the life of the community in which we are – again, doing it from the standpoint of this special relationship.

And then we come to that very difficult thing, the Confession, especially as we use it in the Book of Common Prayer: 'The remembrance of them is grievous unto us; the burden of them is intolerable.' I think that part of the problem about prayer is that we may be thinking of sin as things, we may be thinking of the forgiveness of sins, as opposed to the forgiveness of sinners. And yet, when I think of the burden of the world's wrongness, I think that, again, what we are doing (or at least what I am trying to do in saying the Confession, understanding it corporately) is that we are being representatives of the morality of my station, and we are confessing the shortcomings, the failures, of the morality of my station, that reality in which we are embedded as Christians, forgiven and loved by God.

So we come to the necessity for Christians to recognise in all humility the need of the morality of my station *for* the morality of grace. Now, for many years, I have been interested in the German political philosopher Jürgen Habermas, and he is a very important German political philosopher. A few years ago, at a speech he made in Frankfurt, receiving a prize,[27] he

---

[27] Jürgen Habermas: Speech when receiving the Peace Prize of the German Publishers and Booksellers Association, Paulskirche, Frankfurt, 14 October 2001. See http://www5.csudh.edu/dearhabermas/habermas11.htm.

said something that has been followed up in later writing that, 'Religious traditions are important', and he referred to them as an archive that has resources for modern discussion. This was quite a confession from a man who I don't think has any religious belief, and yet has said some very profound and important things, politically, philosophically, in German life in the post-war period. This has generated an enormous amount of discussion, for which we can only be grateful, because at least in Germany, at any rate, people take seriously religion and theology and the contribution that these things can, or should, make to public life.

But we don't have to go along with Habermas, because in 1940 at the request of Archbishop William Temple (he was then Archbishop of York), the Oxford philosopher A.D. Lindsay wrote the book that I mentioned earlier, entitled *The Two Moralities*. It is such an amazing book that every time I see a second-hand copy I buy it up, so that I can give it or lend it to people. What Lindsay means by the 'two moralities', is what he first of all describes as 'the morality of my station and its duties', a good description of our embeddedness in the social life where we have to trust each other and accept our responsibilities and support our responsibilities. He then goes on to say that there is something that he calls 'the morality of perfection' or 'the morality of grace', which challenges at various points the morality of my station and its duties. Indeed, it is the way in which the morality of grace helps the morality of my station to come to greater and better insights. I want to read a couple of quotations that talk about how he understands the operation of the morality of grace. He says:

> In the morality of my station and its duties, the station presents us with the duty, and we say 'Yes' or 'No.' 'I will' or 'I will not.' We choose between obeying or disobeying a given command. In the morality of challenge or grace the

situation says, 'Here is a mess, a crying evil, a need! What can you do about it?' We are asked not to say 'Yes' or 'No', or 'I will' or 'I will not', but to be inventive, to create, to discover something new. The difference between ordinary people and saints [I'm not sure that I quite like his use of the word 'saints'] is not that saints fulfil the plain duties which ordinary men neglect: the things saints do have not usually occurred to ordinary people at all.[28]

He is therefore talking about what he hopes is going to be within a Christian or religious community, that creativity, that openness to need – I suppose from a Christian point of view we would call it 'love' – that is going to go into situations and is going to transform them through love. And then, right at the very end of the book, he says this:

It is the function of the Church to form a community which is a fellowship, where men can live together in relations governed by a higher standard than prevails in society at large [I would want to translate that as 'in relations governed by the grace of God and that special relationship into which we have been by God's grace called']: to show by the example of her corporate life that the fact that men are all children of one Father is a more effective fact than all their differences of ability and wealth and station. The actual life lived in the Church ought in itself to be a living, effective, and constructive witness against the evils and failures of society. It is also the function of the Church to produce prophets, and the evidence of its vitality will be the fact that it is a school of the prophets: that the men and women who show us what society might do, who correct our blindness and indifference to the evils, are inspired by the Church's fellowship. The Church ought to go a long way to encourage liberty of prophesying, to be prepared to face all the scandal to which liberty of prophesying is bound to give rise.[29]

---

[28] Lindsay, *Two Moralities*, p. 49.
[29] Lindsay, *Two Moralities*, p. 109.

And this, as I say, is coming from a philosopher who was a Christian, but it was a philosophical view of these things; and I would say that this arises from the encounter between forgiven sinners and the world in which they live. In other words, the foolishness of God has a vital part to play in God's world.

APPENDIX 1

Living in the Wilderness
A sermon for Ash Wednesday
14 February 2018

Readings: Deuteronomy 8 and Matthew 4.1-11

> Man shall not live by bread alone, but by every word that proceedeth out of the mouth of the Lord (Matthew 4.4)

The clue to understanding the first of the temptations of Jesus and the Old Testament passage to which he refers in refuting the tempter is contained in the word 'wilderness'. Jesus fasts for forty days and forty nights in the wilderness; the Israelites wandered through the wilderness for forty years on their way from Egypt to the Promised Land.

So what is special and important about 'wilderness'? The important thing is that it is country in which you have to learn to be *dependent* on what the wilderness provides. There aren't any trees to speak of; there aren't any natural resources; it hardly rains; you can't grow anything; you have to be dependent upon the wells and the springs, such as there are; and so you learn in the wilderness to adapt yourself to what is there, to accept gratefully the provision and do what you can with it. In these stories of the Wilderness Wanderings of the

Israelites, there are two ways in which the Israelites are fed, one of which is mentioned in the reading. First, there are the quails, migratory birds that fly between Siberia and North Africa and, twice a year at different seasons, come over the Sinai Wilderness. Some of them through exhaustion and perhaps at the end of their lives come down in the wilderness, and can be collected and used for food. The manna is a substance which is secreted by small insects as they interact with some of the shrubs in the wilderness, and a sticky, sweet substance is exuded which falls to the ground. Given the fact that it is often very cold at night, this substance forms a hard, small disc which can then be used for sweetening purposes; indeed, it is still thus collected and used by the Bedouin.[30] So these are some of the ways in which people subsisting in the wilderness can be fed by the wilderness.

The Wilderness Wanderings traditions in the Old Testament are those very important narratives that stretch from the middle of the Book of Exodus, through Leviticus and Numbers, and then are summed up in Deuteronomy. The picture there is that of a whole nation of thousands of people journeying through the wilderness, something of course that in reality was quite impossible. The historical fact is that Moses led a small group of Israelites from Egypt to the Promised Land through the wilderness, and they *did* depend upon the wilderness. As these stories were told, re-told and embellished (and in many cases converted into some splendid sermons!) the idea that the nation went through the wilderness then had to include with it the idea that the quails and the manna were miraculous acts of God on behalf of his people. In the long run, it doesn't make any difference to the meaning of those stories, because they are about being

---

[30] M. Zohary, *Plants of the Bible*, Cambridge: Cambridge University Press, 1982, pp. 142-3.

dependent, dependent on the wilderness and, in the case of Ancient Israel as a nation, travelling through the wilderness, dependent upon God. This all comes to a head in the magnificent eighth chapter of Deuteronomy: it is because of the need in the wilderness to depend, and, in the case of the Israelites, the need to *learn* to depend upon God, that this chapter becomes so important, especially with its warning:

> Beware that thou forget not the LORD thy God … lest when thou hast eaten and art full, and hast built goodly houses, and dwelt therein, and when thy herds and thy flocks multiply, and thy silver and thy gold is multiplied, and all that thou hast is multiplied; then thine heart be lifted up, and thou forget the LORD thy God, which brought thee forth out of the land of Egypt, from the house of bondage. (Deuteronomy 8.11-14)

In those words there is given one of the most profound definitions of the word 'sin', with which I shall be engaging over the next few weeks in the Beauchief Abbey Lectures. One of the forms that sin takes is the wish, or the action in ignorance, of trying to do without God. Indeed, it takes us back to that primeval story in Genesis 3, where Adam and Eve, representative of the human race, are tempted to do the same, and of course succumb to the temptation. 'Look,' says the tempter to Adam and Eve, 'Look, you don't need God. I know God has said you shouldn't eat the forbidden fruit, but if you eat it you will become like God, you will know good and evil, you won't need to rely on him. Take this step, assert your independence. Do without God.' That is one of the fundamental characteristics of the word that we call 'sin' in one of its many meanings – the desire to do without God, the belief that we can indeed live without God.

This brings me to the first of the three temptations of Jesus. Jesus is in the wilderness for forty days and forty nights, and of course he doesn't go without food and drink for forty days and forty nights; that would be quite impossible, medically and physically. He does, of course, live marginally; he relies on what the wilderness can provide. The tempter comes to him and says, 'Look, you don't need to be relying on what the wilderness provides; you have the power to create your own source of food, so tell these stones to become bread, and then you can feed yourself and you won't need to rely upon what the wilderness supplies, what God supplies through the wilderness.' Jesus, in rebutting what the tempter says, quotes from Deuteronomy: 'Man shall not live by bread only, but by every word that proceedeth out of the mouth of the LORD.'

In the Ancient World, because people did not have written texts, when someone referred to a biblical passage, the assumption would be that they knew the whole of the passage by heart. So in quoting just those words, Jesus is referring to the whole of Deuteronomy 8, with its warning against the Israelites that when they have possessed the Promised Land, and have grown wealthy and rich that they forget God and turn away from him. In the first temptation, Jesus rejects this attempt on the part of the tempter to separate him from God, to get rid of his dependence upon God, to use his powers for his own convenience.

I just want to make three very brief comments arising from this. The first is this: there is nothing wrong with human ambition; there is nothing wrong with human achievement; there is nothing wrong with pride in human achievement, provided that from a Christian point of view those things are set in the context of dependence upon God, that those things are set in a world where we believe that we need God, not that we can do without him. It is within that condition of dependence upon God that there is then the space to use all the intelligence, creativity and initiative that we may possess to try to create a better world and better relationships, but never saying that it is our own might or our own strength that have achieved this.

The second thing I want to say is that within the practice of Judaism, there is each autumn a feast called Sukkot or Booths.[31] It is a remembrance to the Jews of the time when they wandered through the wilderness and were sustained by God's grace and power. And so the observant Jew builds, either on the balcony – lots of them have balconies – or in the garden a booth, made not of substantial materials, but of the sort of thing that you can easily get, shrubs perhaps and small branches. The important thing is that it shouldn't have a really firm roof on it, and that they should sleep in it for seven nights, looking up at the sky above, reminding themselves of the transience of their existence and of their dependence upon God as they wandered through the wilderness. That, I think, is a lovely thing each year, to observe that feast. Now, I am not suggesting that any of us should go and build a *sukkah*, and stay seven nights in it, but we can build a *sukkah* in our imagination, if we want. During my prayers in Lent, I am going to try to think that I am actually in a *sukkah*, a reminder of the transience of it and of dependence upon God – and you might think of doing the same.

The third point is this: in repelling the tempter, Jesus quotes these words, 'Man shall not live by bread only, but by every word that proceedeth out of the mouth of the LORD', and of course we can add to that the words from the New Testament,

---

[31] Y. Vainstein, *The Cycle of the Jewish Year. A Study of the Festivals and of Selections from the Liturgy,* Jerusalem: Department for Torah Education and Culture in the Diaspora, (no date), pp. 93-9.

as well as the Old Testament. Last Sunday morning, for our Epistle, we heard those amazing words from I Corinthians 13:

> Though I speak with the tongues of men and of angels and have not love, I am nothing. (v.1)

The passage lists all the human achievements which, if they are done without love, are worth nothing – and that love is the amazing love that comes from God. But there is far more than that: there are the parables of Jesus, and the Old Testament is replete with passages from God's word, that enable us to get a sense of living in his world. It is not the world as understood and shaped by whatever drives the princes of our press and radio and television, the world as interpreted by them with its emphasis upon bad news, such as this crash or this earthquake or that tragedy, bad as all those things may be and properly as we should take account of them. But that is not the whole of the world. The whole of the world is gathered up in these words that Jesus spoke:

> Man shall not live by bread alone, but by every word that proceeds out of the mouth of the LORD. (Matthew 4:4)

APPENDIX 2

A different perspective
A Sermon for Lent I
18 February 2018

Readings: Genesis 4.1-12 and Hebrews 4.1-16

What do we mean when we say, as we heard in the reading from Hebrews, that 'Christ was in all points tempted like as we are, yet without sin'? In what sense was Jesus without sin? I suppose one way of going about it is to say, Well, sin is when we do, or say, or think wrong things, and therefore if Jesus was without sin, he did not ever think, or do, or say wrong things. Yet there are difficulties about that approach, because when we read the Gospel records, we see Jesus doing things that might well fall under the category of forbidden thoughts, actions and words. We read that Jesus made a cord out of ropes and drove the money-changers out of the Temple, drove their sheep and cattle out of the Temple, overturned their tables and scattered their money. Well now, is that wrongdoing, that sort of violence against people's persons and properties, people going about their lawful, if rather shady, business in the Temple? What about the time when Jesus was aged twelve, and stayed behind in the Temple after his parents had gone home and gave his parents an awful lot of trouble and anxiety, wondering where he was and where he might have got to, and how they had to spend time looking for him? Is that responsible behaviour, for a child to put his parents through that sort of worry and anxiety? What about the occasions when Jesus spoke harshly to people: 'You whited sepulchres!' he said to the Pharisees, accusing them of being only concerned with the outside of the cup, while the inside of the cup was unclean. So, when we look at the actions and words of Jesus, we have to ask ourselves, Was he really without sin in the usual sense of sin as things thought, spoken, done, which are wrong? Of course we might say, Well, perhaps he wasn't without sin; or perhaps we should approach it in a different way.

Now, in our reading from Genesis, the story of Cain and Abel, there occurs a remarkable passage. When God knows that Cain is minded to murder his brother, the Lord says to Cain:

> Why art thou wrath, and why is thy countenance fallen? If thou doest well, shalt thou not be accepted? And if thou doest not well, sin lieth at the door. And unto thee shall be his desire. (Genesis 4.6-7)

Sin here is pictured in the text as a sort of animal, ready to pounce, ready to strike; a negativity that wants to take advantage of the jealousy that Cain feels in his heart, and in that way to incite Cain to do the evil thing of killing his brother. I want us to think for a moment of sin in terms of a massive negativity, a negativity that is often stronger than we are, and which we cannot resist through ignorance or weakness, a negativity with which we sometimes become allies as we are short-tempered, jealous, resentful, intolerant. Towards the first part of Goethe's great play, *Faust,* there come some famous words that express that sense of active negativity marvellously. In one of the first speeches given to the devil Mephistopheles, when Faust wants to know who he is, there come these words in this translation:

> I am the spirit that constantly negates, and rightly so, for everything that comes to me is only fit to perish, wretchedly; 'twere better still if nothing ever saw the light of day, but everything that you call downfall, ruin, sin, is exactly what I take most pleasure in.[32]

And in those famous words there is summed up sin and evil in that sense of an overwhelming negativity. If we think of sin like that, we can truly say that Jesus is without sin in this sense. The whole of the ministry of Jesus is directed positively towards engaging in defeating and overcoming sin in that sense of negativity. Jesus heals the sick, because sickness is a negativity that impairs the life of people. Jesus casts out demons, because whatever demons were, or however we may think of them, the fact that people at the time believed in them was enough to impair the lives that they should have lived. We see Jesus raising the dead, for us a very difficult idea, but notice that two of the raisings of the dead are of children: the daughter of Jaïrus and the son of the Widow of Nain, situations in which negativity has destroyed life for those families, and Jesus works to overcome them. We find Jesus breaking down barriers, which are negative things: he has women disciples and encourages women to follow him, unheard of in the context of the time. He breaks the purity rules, he touches lepers, he associates with sinners, and indeed is criticised for doing that. Anything that Jesus does is aimed towards defeating negativity, and of course the climax comes in those great events to which we build up at the end of Lent – Holy Week and Easter. It is in the events of Holy Week that Jesus confronts the political dishonesty, the misuse of power, the misuse of justice that put an innocent man upon a cross, and subjects him to the most painful death that has been devised. And yet, in confronting death, Jesus overcomes the last enemy, the last enemy that we all sooner or later have to

---

[32] Goethe: *Faust*, Part I, Act 1, lines 1338-1344 (author's translation).

face; and yet, as Christians, we face it in the hope that death has not had the last word, that in Jesus that negativity of all negativities has ultimately been destroyed and overcome.

If we think of the ministry of Jesus in that sense – a ministry of positivity, driven by love – that makes a big difference to how we think in terms of Christianity, and sin, and forgiveness. Christianity is not a life of negative avoidance of faults, with the Church providing some sort of ecclesiastical laundry service where we can get the dirty linen of our moral failures washed clean. It is about responding to the call of Jesus, as when he says to the first disciples, 'Follow me'. It is about embracing, and being embraced by, his offer of the Kingdom, the kingdom of right relationships. It is about trying, within our limitations of weakness and ignorance, to create structures of grace where we are and in all that we do. And when we fail, as we are bound to do, it is because we are doing this in the context of a negativity that is still very much in evidence. And, indeed lately, alas! it is growing in power through the way in which, through electronic social media, young people can be bullied and abused by their peers, and suffer awful distress because of that. We shall fail, and when we fail we go to the One who has triumphed, because, as the reading in Hebrews says, 'He has been tempted like as we are, yet without sin' (Hebrews 4.15). He gives us the courage to go on in his work, and in his might and strength. And so Lent should not be a time of trying to be sad and sorry for ourselves, and trying to give up things. It should be a time of looking out, of branching out, of seeing what opportunities there are, where there are negativities that we can strive against, and in God's power seek to overcome. That, it seems to me, is how from one angle we must think in terms of sin and forgiveness, about which I shall be saying so much in the weeks ahead.

At the end of the Bible, there is that remarkable book, The Revelation of St John the Divine. It is a book that we tend to avoid, because it contains strange things and has been the happy hunting-ground of cranks and millennialists and people telling us when the world is going to end. But in that last book of the Bible, there are more Christian hymns than anywhere else in the New Testament; and it is no accident that when Handel wrote his great oratorio *Messiah*, he took words for two of his greatest choruses from the Book of Revelation: the 'Hallelujah Chorus', and 'Worthy is the Lamb'. In the Book of Revelation we have the worship of the Early Church mirrored, a tiny church, a persecuted church, and yet a church enabled by God's power to see things from the perspective of the divine victory which has been achieved in Jesus Christ.

I want to conclude by reading words from Revelation chapter 5 that sum up the world view from the victory that Christ has won over sin and death and destruction:

> I beheld, and I heard the voice of many angels round about the throne and the living creatures and the elders: and the number of them was ten thousand times ten thousand, and thousands of thousands;
>
> Saying with a loud voice, Worthy is the Lamb that was slain to receive power, and riches, and wisdom, and strength, and honour, and glory, and blessing.
>
> And every creature which is in heaven, and on the earth, and under the earth, and such as are in the sea, and all that are in them, heard I saying, Blessing, and honour, and glory, and power, be unto him that sitteth upon the throne, and unto the Lamb for ever and ever.
>
> And the four living creatures said, Amen. And the four and twenty elders fell down and worshipped him that liveth for ever and ever. (vv. 11-14)

Bibliography

Beattie, J.H.M.,'On Understanding Sacrifice'. In M.F.C. Bourdillon, M. Fortes (eds.), *Sacrifice*, London: Academic Press, 1980, pp. 29-44.

Bourdillon, M.F.C., M. Fortes (eds.), *Sacrifice*, London: Academic Press, 1980.

Brodbeck, K.-H., *Die Herrschaft des Geldes. Geschichte und Systematik*, Darmstadt: Wissenschaftliche Buchgesellschaft, 2009.

Brook, S., *The Language of the Book of Common Prayer*, London: André Deutsch, 1965

Calvin, J., *Institutes of the Christian Religion*, Florida: Macdonald, (no date).

Danby, H., *The Mishnah*, Oxford: Oxford University Press, 1933.

Davies, D., 'An Interpretation of Sacrifice in Leviticus,' *Zeitschrift für die alttestamentliche Wissenschaft* 89 (1977), pp. 387-399.

Dillenberger, J., *Martin Luther. Selections from his Writings*, New York: Anchor Books, 1961.

Habermas, J., Speech on receiving the Peace Prize of the German Publishers and Booksellers Association, Paulskirche, Frankfurt, 14 October 2001. See speech at: http://www5.csudh.edu/dearhabermas/habermas11.htm.

Head, D., *He sent Leanness. A Book of Prayers for the Natural Man*, London: Epworth Press, 1959.

Lindsay, A.D., *The Two Moralities: Our Duty to God and Society*, London: Eyre and Spottiswoode, 1940.

Loades, A., et al. (eds.), *Hermeneutics, the Bible and Literary Criticism*, London: Macmillan, 1992.

Lohmeyer, E., *Das Vater-unser*, Göttingen: Vandenhoeck & Ruprecht, 1947. English version: *The Lord's Prayer*, translated by J. Bowden, London: HarperCollins, 1965.

Lohse, B., *A Short History of Christian Doctrine from the First Century to the Present*, translated by F. Ernest Stoeffler, Philadelphia: Fortress Press, 1963.

Manson, T.W., *On Paul and John: Some Selected Theological Themes*. Studies in Biblical Theology No 38, London: SCM Press, 1963.

Manson, T.W., *The Sayings of Jesus as Recorded in the Gospels according to St Matthew and St Luke*, London: SCM Press, 1950.

Maurice, F.D., *The Patriarchs and Lawgivers of the Old Testament. A Series of Sermons Preached in the Chapel of Lincoln's Inn,* London: Macmillan, 1892.

Maurice, F.D., *The Kingdom of Christ,* 2 vols, London: James Clarke (reprint), 1959.

Mishnah Tractate *Yoma* 6.6, in H. Danby, *The Mishnah,* Oxford: Oxford University Press, 1933, p. 170.

Moffatt, J., *The New Testament: A New Translation in Modern Speech (based on the Greek text by von Soden),* London: Hodder and Stoughton, 1913, Revised 1917.

Quick, O.C., *The Realism of Christ's Parables,* London: SCM Press, 1952

Quick, O.C, *Doctrines of the Creed. Their Basis in Scripture and Their Meaning Today,* London: Nisbet & Co., 1938,

Rogerson, J.W., *Cultural Landscapes and the Bible. Collected Essays,* Sheffield: Beauchief Abbey Press, 2014.

Rogerson, J.W., *Perspectives on the Passion,* Sheffield: Beauchief Abbey Press, 2014.

Rogerson, J.W., 'Sacrifice in the Old Testament. Problems of Method and Approach'. In M.F.C. Bourdillon, M. Fortes (eds.), *Sacrifice,* London: Academic Press, 1980, pp. 45-60. Reprinted in J. W. Rogerson, *Cultural Landscapes and the Bible. Collected Essays,* Sheffield: Beauchief Abbey Press, 2014, pp. 72-92.

Rogerson, J.W., 'Wrestling with the Angel. A Study in Literary Hermeneutics' in A. Loades et al. (eds.), *Hermeneutics, the Bible and Literary Criticism,* London: Macmillan, 1992, pp. 131-144. Reprinted in J. W. Rogerson, *Cultural Landscapes and the Bible.* Sheffield: Beauchief Abbey Press, 2014. pp. 285-302.

Sayings of the Jewish Fathers (Pirke Aboth).

Temple, W., *Christianity and Social Order,* Harmondsworth: Penguin, 1942.

Y. Vainstein, *The Cycle of the Jewish Year. A Study of the Festivals and of Selections from the Liturgy,* Jerusalem: Department for Torah Education and Culture in the Diaspora, (no date).

Vermes, G., *The Complete Dead Sea Scrolls in English,* London: Penguin (7th Edition), 2011.

Westcott, B.F., *The Epistle to the Hebrews: The Greek Text with Notes and Essays,* London: Macmillan, 1892.

Zohary, M. *Plants of the Bible,* Cambridge: Cambridge University Press, 1982.

Biblical References

OLD TESTAMENT		Psalms		Luke (contd)	
Genesis	33	30		15.4-10	51
3	84	32	56	15.11-32	42, 49
4	20, 64, 89	51	37	16.1-9	42
4.1-12	88, 89	98.7-9	60	18.9-14	51
12.1-2	34	103.12	29	19.11-27	42
12.9-20	34	103.13-17	38-9	21.38	48
16.1-3	34	136	37	John	
20.1-18	34	Isaiah		7.53-8.11	48
28.10-22	34	1.2	38	10	19
32.9-12	35	1.2-3	43	Romans	
32.23-32	34	11	56, 66	1.18	60
Exodus	36, 83	53.6	18	1.25	61
2.1-10	35	64.6	70	5.6-8	59, 65
3.1-20	35	65	56, 66	7.18-25	64, 65
22.25	22	Jeremiah		8.22	56
23.10-12	21	2.13	43	8.38	63
34	32	23.1-4	19	I Corinthians	
Leviticus	36, 83	Ezekiel		1.23-5	59
6.1, 7	30	34	19	13.1	87
16	32	Micah		13.4-8	72-3
17.10-14	31	7.18-19	38	15.10	67
19.20	30			II Corinthians	
25	23	NEW TESTAMENT		3.6	62
Numbers	32, 36, 83	Matthew	41	5.17	57
16	32	4.4	82, 87	5.19	58
19	31	4.1-11	88	6.8-10	67
Deuteronomy	36	5.43-8	73	Galatians	
8	82, 84	6.12	40	2.20	59, 67
15	23	18.23-35	42, 45	3.21	62
I Samuel		25.14-30	42	3.28	57
13.14	37	Mark		5.22	63
25.29	45	1.15	66	Colossians	
II Samuel		2.1-12	49	1.13	56
11	37	2.27	62	Hebrews	30
12.13	37	Luke	41	4.1-16	88, 91
		7.36-50	42	Revelation	
		11.4	41	5	92

Index

Abraham narratives 33-4
Adam and Eve 84
Amish 73-4
Ancient Egypt 16, 18
Ancient Israel and sacrifice 7, 31-3
Ancient World 18, 85
Apostles' Creed 15, 26, 27-8, 69, 76
Atonement, the 59
Barrett, C.K. 72
Beattie, J.H.M. 31
blood as factor in sacrifice 31-3
Book of Common Prayer 17, 18, 77, 78
Book of the Dead 16
Booths, Feast of 86
Brook, S. 18
Cain and Abel 20, 64, 89
Calvin, J. 25-6
Calvinism 36
Chartism 23
Christian lifestyle 23-7
Church, as community 80
Church, one-dimensional 67-8, 71-2
Confession (BCP) 17, 78
covenant relationship 32, 36-7, 39
Cross, significance of the 27, 29, 44, 62-3, 90-91
Cross, First Word from the 47-8
Danby, H. 33
David narratives 33, 37-8
Davies, D. 33
Day of Atonement 32-3
Dead Sea Scrolls 63

dependence on God 42-3, 84-6
Dillenberger, J. 39
Early Church 62, 68, 72, 92
environment, care of 21-2
eschatology 56, 66, 67
Eucharist 77
General Confession (BCP) 17-18, 19, 26-7
God's holy laws 21-3, 26
Goethe 89-90
grace, dimension of 56, 57, 67, 73, 74
Habermas, J. 78-9
Handel's *Messiah* 18, 92
Head, D. 26-7
Holy Spirit 63, 66, 71-2
Jacob narratives 33, 34-5
Jaïrus's daughter 90
judgement and the law 60-63, 75
justification by faith 59-60, 72, 77
Kingdom of God 23-4, 55-60, 66, 70-72, 91
Kingsley, C. 23
liminal events and sacrifice 30-32
Lindsay, A.D. 74, 79-81
Liturgical Year 76-7
Loades, A. 35
Lohmeyer, E. 41-3
Lord's Prayer 40-41, 45-6
love (*agape*) 72-3, 87, 91
Luhmann, N. 46
Luther, M. 39, 40, 70
Manson, T.W. 51-2, 58
Maurice, F.D. 23-4
Montanists 68, 72

Moralities, the Two 74, 79-80
morality of grace 50-52, 53, 78-80
Moses narratives 33, 35-6, 83
Parable of the –
　Dishonest Steward 42
　Lost Coin 51-2
　Lost Sheep 51-2
　Pharisee and Publican 51
　Pounds 42
　Prodigal Son 42, 49-51, 58
　Talents 42
　Two Debtors 42
　Unforgiving Servant 42, 45
paralysed man, healing of 49
parousia 67-8
penal substitution 44
penitent thief 52-3
Phillips, J.B. 47
prophetic books 30, 38, 43
Psalms and forgiveness 29-30, 37-8
Quick, O. 16, 52
Rogerson, J.W. 31, 35
Sabbath observance 21-2, 62
sacrificial system 30-33, 36
sheep and shepherds 18-20
Simeon the Just 61
sin, definition of 17, 84
sins and sinners, compared 17, 69-71, 76-8
Temple, W. 24, 79
Temptations of Jesus 82, 84-6
Ten Commandments 21, 25-6
Third World debt 23
trespasses and debts 40-4
Tutu, D. 75
Tyndale, W. 40-41
Lohse, B. 41
usury and interest 22-3, 24
Vainstein, Y 86
Westcott, B.F. 30, 32
Widow of Nain 90

Wilderness Wanderings 36-7, 82-5
Wink, W. 64
woman taken in adultery 48
worship 38, 61-2, 75, 92
Zohary, M. 83

Also by J.W. Rogerson

*The Gift of Repentance
and other Sermons* (2018)

*Jochen Klepper (1903-1942)
Christian Poet and Witness in Troubled Times* (2018)

The Poet Prophets of the Old Testament (2018)

The Case for Ernst Lohmeyer (2017)

*Upside-Down Kingdom
Beauchief Abbey Sermons 2012-2015* (2015)

*Cultural Landscapes and the Bible
Collected Essays* (2015)

*The Kingdom of God
Five Lectures* (2015)

Perspectives on the Passion (2014)

*The Holy Spirit in Biblical and
Pastoral Perspective* (2013)

*On Being a Broad Church
An Exploration* (2013)

Published by Beauchief Abbey Press
and available from www.lulu.com

www.ingramcontent.com/pod-product-compliance
Lightning Source LLC
LaVergne TN
LVHW051527070426
835507LV00023B/3340